TO JAMES AND WEI

WISHING ALL THE BEST TO BOTH OF YOU

AND TAKE CARE, ENJOY BAKING ALWAYS.

FROM:
"O" AND "G"
BERMUDA.
5/1/93.

HERSHEY'S® FABULOUS DESSERTS

PUBLICATIONS INTERNATIONAL, LTD.

All recipes developed and tested by the Hershey Kitchens.

Pictured on the front cover: Chocolatetown Special Cake (*see page 58*).

Pictured on the back cover, on the left: Fudge Brownie Pie (*see page 93*).
On the right (*top to bottom*): Reese's Chewy Chocolate Cookies and Hershey's Great American Chocolate Chip Cookies (*see page 164*), Chocolate Cherry Upside-Down Cake (*see page 45*), and Chocolate Mint Dessert (*see page 62*).

Microwave cooking times given in this book are approximate. Numerous variables, such as the microwave oven's rated wattage and starting temperature, shape, amount and depth of the food, can affect cooking time. Use the cooking times as a guideline and check doneness before adding more time. Lower wattage ovens may consistently require longer cooking times.

Library of Congress Catalog Card Number: 89-60930

ISBN: 0-88176-677-1

This edition published by Publications International, Ltd.,
7373 N. Cicero Avenue, Lincolnwood, IL 60646

If you have any questions or comments about the recipes in this book, or about any of our fine Hershey products, please write us at The Hershey Kitchens, P.O. Box 815, Hershey, PA 17033-0815, or call us, toll-free, weekdays 9am–4pm Eastern time, at 1-800-468-1714.

Printed and bound in United States by Arcata Graphics/Hawkins

h g f e d c

Contents

FABULOUS DESSERTS

What comes to mind when you think about chocolate? Perhaps it's chocolate's irresistibly rich and luxurious flavor. That's why millions of us across the country are devoted chocolate lovers. Milton S. Hershey was devoted to chocolate too. When he made his first milk chocolate bar in 1894, little did he know that Hershey would become "America's Chocolate Authority"™.

Today Hershey offers a rich heritage in fine quality chocolates from HERSHEY'S milk chocolate bars and HERSHEY'S KISSES chocolates to the very best for baking with HERSHEY'S cocoa, chocolate chips and baking chocolate. What better way to enjoy the very best chocolate desserts than with Hershey's!

If you've made a batch of Great American Chocolate Chip Cookies from the recipe found on every bag of HERSHEY'S chocolate chips, or seen a recipe in your favorite magazine, then you're familiar with the kind of work we do in the Hershey Kitchens. For over 30 years, we've been developing new chocolate snacks and desserts for all occasions as well as updating popular classics to fit today's lifestyles.

The *HERSHEY'S Fabulous Chocolate Recipes* cookbook has been designed for all chocolate-loving cooks. The key ingredient in all our recipes is chocolate, of course, and 100% pure HERSHEY'S, too. The easy-to-follow recipe instructions and special hints throughout will help

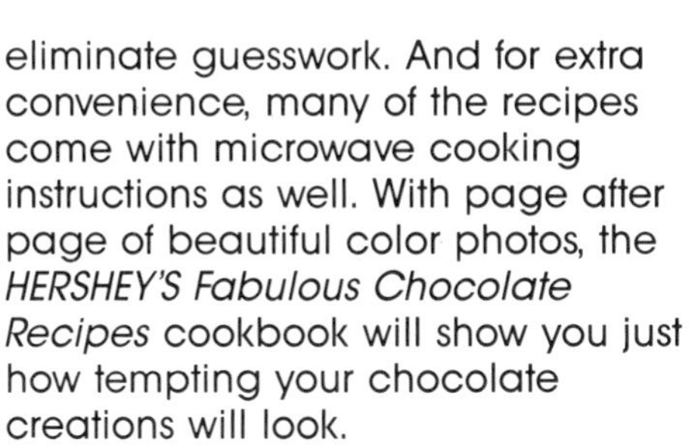

eliminate guesswork. And for extra convenience, many of the recipes come with microwave cooking instructions as well. With page after page of beautiful color photos, the *HERSHEY'S Fabulous Chocolate Recipes* cookbook will show you just how tempting your chocolate creations will look.

Turn the pages and find popular Hershey classics and tantalizing new desserts that are quick, easy and taste like you've baked all day! From everyday family favorites and chocolate snacking treats to elegant endings and indulgent rewards, *HERSHEY'S Fabulous Chocolate Recipes* was designed to make your dessert selections easier and better than ever before.

The Hershey Kitchens

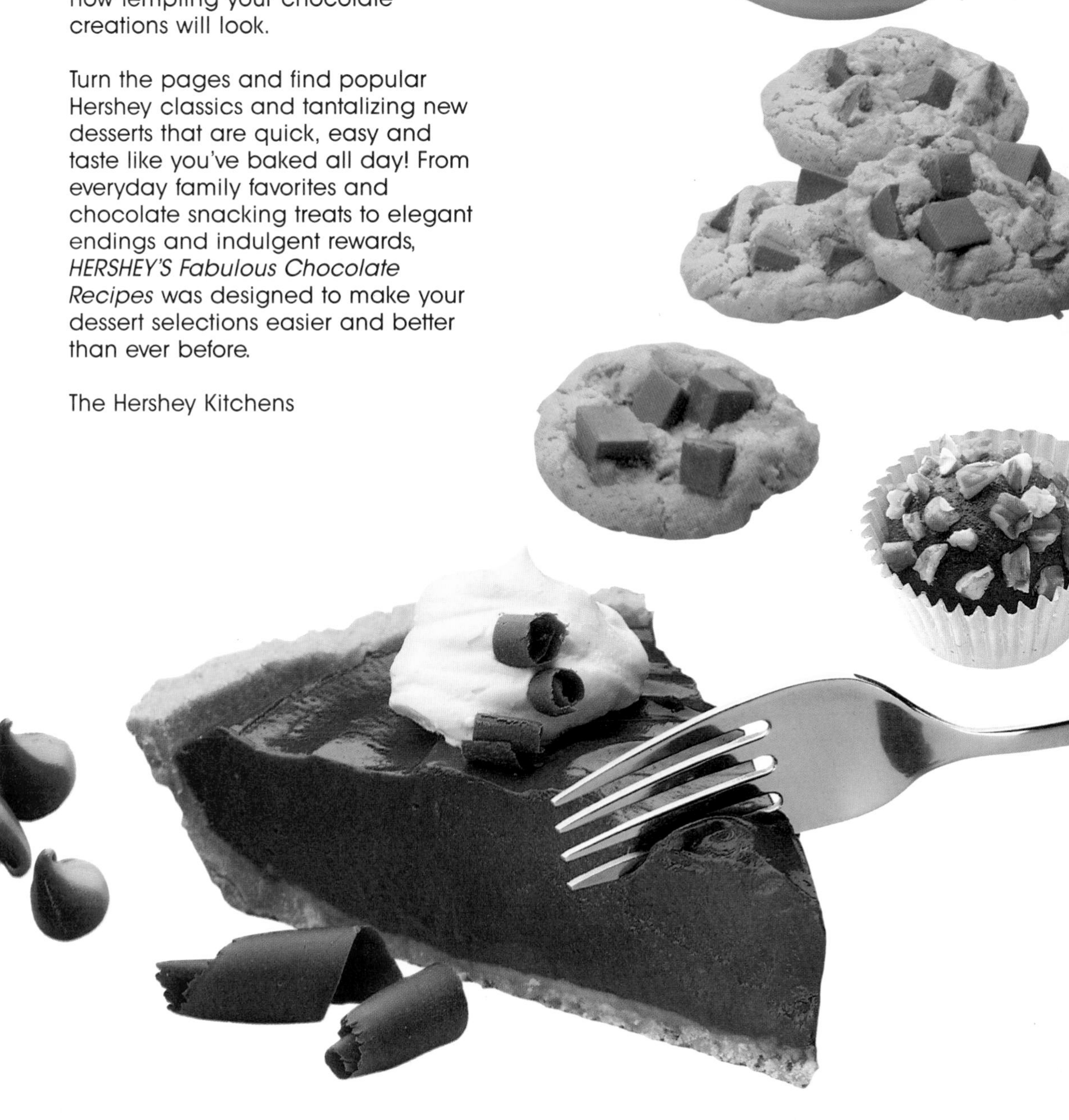

CAKES & CHEESECAKES

From elegant to easy, indulge yourself with any one of these wonderful cakes.

From left to right: Devil's Delight Cake, Peanut Butter-Fudge Marble Cake (recipes page 8) and Chocolate Sour Cream Cake (recipe page 9).

Devil's Delight Cake

1 package (18.25 ounces) devil's food cake mix (with pudding in the mix)
4 eggs
1 cup water
1/2 cup vegetable oil
1 cup chopped nuts
1 cup miniature marshmallows
1 cup HERSHEY'S Semi-Sweet Chocolate Chips
1/2 cup raisins
Confectioners' sugar or Chocolate Chip Glaze (recipe follows)

Heat oven to 350°. Grease and flour 12-cup Bundt pan. In large mixer bowl combine cake mix, eggs, water and oil; beat on low speed just until blended. Increase speed to medium; beat 2 minutes. Stir in nuts, marshmallows, chocolate chips and raisins. Pour batter into prepared pan. Bake 45 to 50 minutes or until wooden pick inserted in center comes out clean. Cool 10 minutes; remove from pan to wire rack. Cool completely. Sprinkle confectioners' sugar over top or drizzle Chocolate Chip Glaze over top.

12 to 16 servings

Chocolate Chip Glaze

In small saucepan combine 2 tablespoons butter or margarine, 2 tablespoons light corn syrup and 2 tablespoons water. Cook over low heat, stirring constantly, until mixture begins to boil. Remove from heat; add 1 cup HERSHEY'S Semi-Sweet Chocolate Chips. Stir until chips are melted and mixture is smooth. Continue stirring until glaze is desired consistency.

About 1 cup glaze

Peanut Butter-Fudge Marble Cake

1 package (18.25 or 19.75 ounces) fudge marble cake mix
3 eggs
1/3 cup plus 2 tablespoons vegetable oil, divided
Water
1 cup REESE'S Peanut Butter Chips

Heat oven to 350°. Grease and flour two 8 or 9-inch round baking pans. Prepare cake batters according to package directions using eggs, 1/3 cup oil and water. In top of double boiler over hot, not boiling, water melt peanut butter chips with remaining 2 tablespoons oil, stirring constantly. OR, in small microwave-safe bowl place chips and oil. Microwave at HIGH (100%) 45 seconds; stir. (If necessary, microwave at HIGH additional 15 seconds or until melted and smooth when stirred.) Gradually add peanut butter mixture to vanilla batter, blending well. Pour peanut butter batter into prepared pans. Randomly place spoonfuls of chocolate batter on top; swirl as directed on package. Bake 30 to 40 minutes or until wooden pick inserted in center comes out clean. Cool 15 minutes; remove from pans. Cool completely on wire rack; frost as desired.

10 to 12 servings

Chocolate Sour Cream Cake

- 1 3/4 cups all-purpose flour
- 1 3/4 cups sugar
- 3/4 cup HERSHEY'S Cocoa
- 1 1/2 teaspoons baking soda
- 1 teaspoon salt
- 2/3 cup butter or margarine, softened
- 2 cups dairy sour cream
- 2 eggs
- 1 teaspoon vanilla extract
- Fudge Frosting (recipe follows)

Heat oven to 350°. Grease and flour 13×9×2-inch baking pan. In large mixer bowl combine flour, sugar, cocoa, baking soda and salt. Blend in butter, sour cream, eggs and vanilla. Beat 3 minutes on medium speed. Pour batter into prepared pan. Bake 40 to 45 minutes or until wooden pick inserted in center comes out clean. Cool in pan on wire rack. Frost with Fudge Frosting.

12 to 15 servings

Fudge Frosting

- 3 tablespoons butter or margarine
- 1/3 cup HERSHEY'S Cocoa
- 1 1/3 cups confectioners' sugar
- 2 to 3 tablespoons milk
- 1/2 teaspoon vanilla extract

In small saucepan over low heat melt butter. Add cocoa; cook, stirring constantly, just until mixture begins to boil. Pour mixture into small mixer bowl; cool completely. To cocoa mixture, add confectioners' sugar alternately with milk, beating to spreading consistency. Blend in vanilla.

About 1 cup frosting

Hot Fudge Pudding Cake

- 1 1/4 cups granulated sugar, divided
- 1 cup all-purpose flour
- 7 tablespoons HERSHEY'S Cocoa, divided
- 2 teaspoons baking powder
- 1/4 teaspoon salt
- 1/2 cup milk
- 1/3 cup butter or margarine, melted
- 1 1/2 teaspoons vanilla extract
- 1/2 cup packed light brown sugar
- 1 1/4 cups hot water

Heat oven to 350°. In medium bowl combine 3/4 cup granulated sugar, flour, 3 tablespoons cocoa, baking powder and salt. Blend in milk, butter and vanilla; beat until smooth. Pour batter into 8- or 9-inch square baking pan. In small bowl combine remaining 1/2 cup granulated sugar, brown sugar and remaining 4 tablespoons cocoa; sprinkle mixture evenly over batter. Pour water over top; *do not stir.* Bake 35 to 40 minutes or until center is almost set. Let stand 15 minutes; spoon into dessert dishes, spooning sauce from bottom of pan over top. Garnish as desired.

8 to 10 servings

Hot Fudge Pudding Cake

Marbled Angel Cake

1 box (14.5 ounces) angel food cake mix
1/4 cup HERSHEY'S Cocoa
Chocolate Glaze (recipe follows)

Adjust oven rack to lowest position. Heat oven to 375°. Prepare cake batter according to package directions. Measure 4 cups batter into separate bowl; gradually fold cocoa into this batter until well blended, being careful not to deflate batter. Alternately pour vanilla and chocolate batters into ungreased 10-inch tube pan. Cut through batter with knife or spatula to marble batter. Bake 30 to 35 minutes or until top crust is firm and looks very dry. Do not underbake. Invert pan on heat-proof funnel or bottle; cool at least 1 1/2 hours. Carefully run knife along side of pan to loosen cake. Place on serving plate; drizzle with Chocolate Glaze.

12 to 16 servings

Chocolate Glaze

In small saucepan bring 1/3 cup sugar and 1/4 cup water to full boil, stirring until sugar dissolves. Remove from heat; add 1 cup HERSHEY'S MINI CHIPS Semi-Sweet Chocolate. Stir with wire whisk until chips are melted and mixture is smooth. Cool to desired consistency; use immediately.

About 2/3 cup glaze

Chocolate Cake with Crumb Topping

Crumb Topping (recipe follows)
1 1/2 cups all-purpose flour
1 cup sugar
1/4 cup HERSHEY'S Cocoa
1 teaspoon baking soda
1/2 teaspoon salt
1 cup water
1/4 cup plus 2 tablespoons vegetable oil
1 tablespoon white vinegar
1 teaspoon vanilla extract
Whipped topping or ice cream (optional)

Prepare Crumb Topping; set aside. Heat oven to 350°. Grease and flour 9-inch square baking pan. In medium bowl combine flour, sugar, cocoa, baking soda and salt. Add water, oil, vinegar and vanilla; beat with spoon or wire whisk just until batter is smooth and ingredients are well blended. Pour batter into prepared pan. Sprinkle topping over batter. Bake 35 minutes or until wooden pick inserted in center comes out clean. Cool in pan on wire rack. Serve with whipped topping or ice cream, if desired.

About 9 servings

Crumb Topping

In small bowl combine 1/2 cup graham cracker crumbs, 1/4 cup chopped nuts and 2 tablespoons melted butter or margarine. Stir in 1/2 cup HERSHEY'S Semi-Sweet Chocolate Chips.

Marbled Angel Cake (top) and Chocolate Cake with Crumb Topping

Filled Rich Chocolate Cupcakes

Filling (recipe follows)
3 cups all-purpose flour
2 cups sugar
2/3 cup HERSHEY'S Cocoa
2 teaspoons baking soda
1 teaspoon salt
2 cups water
2/3 cup vegetable oil
2 tablespoons white vinegar
2 teaspoons vanilla extract

Prepare Filling; set aside. Heat oven to 350°. In large mixer bowl combine flour, sugar, cocoa, baking soda and salt. Add water, oil, vinegar and vanilla; beat on medium speed 2 minutes or until well combined. Fill paper-lined muffin cups (2 1/2 inches in diameter) 2/3 full with batter. Spoon 1 level tablespoon Filling into center of each cupcake. Bake 20 to 25 minutes or until wooden pick inserted in cake portion comes out clean. Remove to wire rack. Cool completely.

About 2 1/2 dozen cupcakes

Filling

1 package (8 ounces) cream cheese, softened
1/3 cup sugar
1 egg
1/8 teaspoon salt
1 cup HERSHEY'S Semi-Sweet Chocolate Chips or MINI CHIPS Chocolate

In small mixer bowl combine cream cheese, sugar, egg and salt; beat until smooth and creamy. Stir in chocolate chips.

VARIATIONS
Goblin's Delight Filling: Add 2 teaspoons grated orange peel, 4 drops yellow food color and 3 drops red food color to Filling before stirring in chips.

Valentine Filling: Add 4 to 5 drops red food color to Filling.

No-Bake Chocolate Cheesecake

- 1 1/2 cups HERSHEY'S Semi-Sweet Chocolate Chips
- 1 package (8 ounces) cream cheese, softened
- 1 package (3 ounces) cream cheese, softened
- 1/2 cup sugar
- 1/4 cup butter or margarine, softened
- 2 cups frozen non-dairy whipped topping, thawed
- 8-inch (6 ounces) packaged graham cracker crumb crust

Microwave Directions: In small microwave-safe bowl place chocolate chips. Microwave at HIGH (100%) 1 to 1 1/2 minutes or until chips are melted and mixture is smooth when stirred. Set aside to cool. In large mixer bowl beat cream cheese, sugar and butter until smooth. On low speed blend in melted chocolate. Fold in whipped topping until blended; spoon into crust. Cover; chill until firm. Garnish as desired. *About 8 servings*

Hershey's Chocolate Peppermint Log

- 4 eggs, separated
- 1/2 cup plus 1/3 cup granulated sugar, divided
- 1 teaspoon vanilla extract
- 1/2 cup all-purpose flour
- 1/3 cup HERSHEY'S Cocoa
- 1/2 teaspoon baking powder
- 1/4 teaspoon baking soda
- 1/8 teaspoon salt
- 1/3 cup water
- Confectioners' sugar
- Peppermint Filling (recipe follows)
- Chocolate Glaze (recipe follows)

Heat oven to 375°. Line 15 1/2 × 10 1/2 × 1-inch jelly-roll pan with aluminum foil; generously grease foil. In large mixer bowl beat egg whites until foamy; gradually add 1/2 cup granulated sugar, beating until stiff peaks form. Set aside. In small mixer bowl beat egg yolks and vanilla on high speed about 3 minutes; gradually add remaining 1/3 cup granulated sugar. Continue beating 2 additional minutes. Combine flour, cocoa, baking powder, baking soda and salt; add to egg yolk mixture alternately with water on low speed, beating just until batter is smooth. Gradually fold chocolate mixture into egg whites; spread evenly in prepared pan. Bake 12 to 15 minutes or until top springs back when touched lightly in center.

Immediately loosen cake from edges of pan; invert on towel sprinkled with confectioners' sugar. Carefully remove foil. Immediately roll cake in towel starting from narrow end; place on wire rack to cool. Prepare Peppermint Filling. Unroll cake; remove towel. Spread with filling; reroll cake. Glaze with Chocolate Glaze; chill. Garnish as desired.

10 to 12 servings

Peppermint Filling

In small mixer bowl beat 1 cup chilled whipping cream until slightly thickened. Add 1/4 cup confectioners' sugar and 1/4 cup finely crushed hard peppermint candy or 1/2 teaspoon mint extract and a few drops red food color, if desired; beat until stiff.

Chocolate Glaze

2 tablespoons butter or margarine
2 tablespoons HERSHEY'S Cocoa
2 tablespoons water
1/2 teaspoon vanilla extract
1 cup confectioners' sugar

In small saucepan over low heat melt butter. Add cocoa and water, stirring until smooth and slightly thickened; *do not boil*. Remove from heat; cool slightly. Add vanilla. (Cool completely for thicker, frosting-type topping.) Gradually add confectioners' sugar, beating with wire whisk until smooth.

About 3/4 cup glaze

Chocolate Zucchini Cake

- 3 eggs
- 1 1/2 cups sugar
- 1 teaspoon vanilla extract
- 1/2 cup vegetable oil
- 2 cups all-purpose flour
- 1/3 cup HERSHEY'S Cocoa
- 1 teaspoon baking powder
- 1 teaspoon baking soda
- 1 teaspoon ground cinnamon
- 1/4 teaspoon salt
- 3/4 cup buttermilk or sour milk*
- 2 cups coarsely shredded raw zucchini
- 1 cup chopped nuts
- 1/2 cup raisins
- Creamy Chocolate Chip Glaze (recipe follows)

Heat oven to 350°. Grease and flour 12-cup Bundt pan. In large mixer bowl beat eggs. Gradually add sugar and vanilla, beating until thick and light in color. Gradually pour in oil, beating until blended. Combine flour, cocoa, baking powder, baking soda, cinnamon and salt; add alternately with buttermilk to egg mixture. Drain zucchini well; fold into batter. Stir in nuts and raisins; pour into prepared pan. Bake 55 to 60 minutes or until wooden pick inserted in center comes out clean. Cool 10 minutes; invert onto serving plate. Cool completely. Glaze with Creamy Chocolate Chip Glaze. Garnish as desired. *12 servings*

*To sour milk: Use 2 teaspoons white vinegar plus milk to equal 3/4 cup.

Creamy Chocolate Chip Glaze

- 2 tablespoons sugar
- 2 tablespoons water
- 1/2 cup HERSHEY'S Semi-Sweet Chocolate Chips or MINI CHIPS
- 1 tablespoon marshmallow creme
- 1 to 2 teaspoons hot water

In small saucepan combine sugar and 2 tablespoons water; bring to boil. Remove from heat; immediately add chocolate chips and stir until melted. Blend in marshmallow creme. Add hot water, 1/2 teaspoon at a time, until glaze is desired consistency. *About 1/2 cup glaze*

Ice Cream Sundae Cake

- 1 package (18.25 to 18.75 ounces) cake mix, any flavor
- 1 can (16 ounces) HERSHEY'S Chocolate Fudge Topping, at room temperature
- Ice Cream

Prepare and bake cake according to package directions for 13 × 9 × 2-inch baking pan. Remove from oven; immediately place heaping tablespoonfuls of fudge topping on cake. Let stand 15 minutes or until fudge topping is soft enough to spread. Gently spread evenly over cake. Serve slightly warm or cool, with scoops of ice cream.

12 to 15 servings

Chocolate Zucchini Cake

Deep Dark Chocolate Cake

Deep Dark Chocolate Cake

- 2 cups sugar
- $1\frac{3}{4}$ cups all-purpose flour
- $\frac{3}{4}$ cup HERSHEY'S Cocoa
- $1\frac{1}{2}$ teaspoons baking powder
- $1\frac{1}{2}$ teaspoons baking soda
- 1 teaspoon salt
- 2 eggs
- 1 cup milk
- $\frac{1}{2}$ cup vegetable oil
- 2 teaspoons vanilla extract
- 1 cup boiling water
- One-Bowl Buttercream Frosting (recipe page 191)

Heat oven to 350°. Grease and flour two 9-inch round baking pans or 13 × 9 × 2-inch baking pan. In large mixer bowl combine sugar, flour, cocoa, baking powder, baking soda and salt. Add eggs, milk, oil and vanilla; beat on medium speed 2 minutes. Remove from mixer; stir in boiling water (batter will be thin). Pour into prepared pan(s). Bake 30 to 35 minutes for round pans, 35 to 40 minutes for rectangular pan, or until wooden pick inserted in center comes out clean. Cool 10 minutes; remove from pan(s) to wire rack. Cool completely. (Cake may be left in rectangular pan, if desired.) Frost with One-Bowl Buttercream Frosting.

8 to 10 servings

VARIATION

Chocolate Cupcakes: Prepare Deep Dark Chocolate Cake as directed. Fill paper-lined muffin cups ($2\frac{1}{2}$ inches in diameter) $\frac{2}{3}$ full with batter. Bake at 350° for 18 to 22 minutes or until wooden pick inserted in center comes out clean. Cool; frost as desired.

About 3 dozen cupcakes

Peanut Butter Pudding Cake

- 1 package (13.5 ounces) applesauce raisin snack cake mix
- $2\frac{1}{4}$ cups water, divided
- 2 cups (12-ounce package) REESE'S Peanut Butter Chips, divided
- $1\frac{1}{3}$ cups packed light brown sugar
- 1 tablespoon butter or margarine
- 1 tablespoon lemon juice
- Whipped topping

Heat oven to 350°. In 9-inch square baking pan combine cake mix and 1 cup water. Mix with fork until smooth. Stir in 1 cup peanut butter chips. Sprinkle remaining 1 cup chips over batter. In medium saucepan combine brown sugar, remaining $1\frac{1}{4}$ cups water, butter and lemon juice. Stir constantly over medium heat until mixture boils. Pour hot mixture over batter in pan; *do not stir.* Bake 45 minutes. Cool 15 minutes. Spoon into dessert dishes, spooning sauce from bottom of pan over top. Serve with whipped topping.

About 8 servings

Collector's Cocoa Cake

Collector's Cocoa Cake

- 3/4 cup butter or margarine
- 1 3/4 cups sugar
- 2 eggs
- 1 teaspoon vanilla extract
- 2 cups all-purpose flour
- 3/4 cup HERSHEY'S Cocoa
- 1 1/4 teaspoons baking soda
- 1/2 teaspoon salt
- 1 1/3 cups water
- Peanut Butter Cream Frosting (recipe follows)

Heat oven to 350°. Grease and flour two 8- or 9-inch round baking pans. In large mixer bowl cream butter and sugar. Add eggs and vanilla; beat 1 minute at medium speed. Combine flour, cocoa, baking soda and salt; add alternately with water to creamed mixture, beating after each addition. Pour batter into prepared pans. Bake 35 to 40 minutes for 8-inch rounds, 30 to 35 minutes for 9-inch rounds, or until wooden pick inserted in center comes out clean. Cool 10 minutes; remove from pans. Cool completely. Frost with Peanut Butter Cream Frosting. Cover; refrigerate frosted cake. *8 to 10 servings*

Peanut Butter Cream Frosting

- 2 cups (12-ounce package) REESE'S Peanut Butter Chips
- 2/3 cup milk
- 3 cups miniature marshmallows
- 2 cups chilled whipping cream
- 1/2 teaspoon vanilla extract

In top of double boiler over hot, not boiling, water combine peanut butter chips, milk and marshmallows. Stir until marshmallows and chips are melted and mixture is smooth. Cool to lukewarm. In large mixer bowl beat cream and vanilla until stiff; fold in cooled peanut butter mixture. *About 5 cups frosting*

Celebration Chocolate Cake

- 3/4 cup HERSHEY'S Cocoa
- 1 cup boiling water
- 1/2 cup plus 2 tablespoons butter or margarine
- 2 cups sugar
- 3 eggs
- 1 teaspoon vanilla extract
- 1 3/4 cups all-purpose flour
- 1 1/2 teaspoons baking soda
- 1/4 teaspoon salt
- 3/4 cup milk
- 1/4 cup dairy sour cream
- Celebration Chocolate Frosting (recipe follows)

Heat oven to 350°. Grease three 9-inch round baking pans. Line bottoms with wax paper; grease and flour paper. In small bowl mix cocoa with boiling water; stir until smooth. Set aside to cool. In large mixer bowl cream butter and sugar until light and fluffy. Add eggs, one at a time, beating well after each addition. Stir in vanilla. Gradually add cocoa mixture; blend well. Combine flour, baking soda and salt; add alternately with milk and sour cream to creamed mixture. Pour batter into prepared pans. Bake 30 to 35 minutes or until wooden pick inserted in center comes out clean. Cool 10 minutes. Remove from pans; carefully peel off paper. Cool completely. Frost with Celebration Chocolate Frosting. Cover; refrigerate frosted cake.

10 to 12 servings

Celebration Chocolate Frosting

- 1/2 cup butter or margarine
- 3/4 cup HERSHEY'S Cocoa
- 2 3/4 cups confectioners' sugar
- 1/2 cup milk, heated slightly
- 1 teaspoon vanilla extract
- 1 egg yolk

In small saucepan over low heat melt butter; add cocoa. Continue to cook, stirring constantly, until smooth. Pour into large mixer bowl; cool to room temperature. Add confectioners' sugar alternately with milk, beating until smooth and of desired consistency. Blend in vanilla and egg yolk; beat well.

About 2 1/4 cups frosting

Cocoa-Cola Cake

- 2 cups sugar
- 2 cups all-purpose flour
- 1/2 cup vegetable oil
- 1/2 cup butter or margarine
- 1/3 cup HERSHEY'S Cocoa
- 1 cup cola (not diet)
- 1/2 cup buttermilk or sour milk*
- 1 teaspoon baking soda
- 2 eggs, slightly beaten
- 1 teaspoon vanilla extract
- 1 1/2 cups miniature marshmallows
- Chocolate Nut Frosting (recipe follows)

Heat oven to 350°. Grease 13×9×2-inch baking pan. In large mixer bowl combine sugar and flour; set aside. In medium saucepan combine oil, butter, cocoa and cola. Cook over medium heat, stirring constantly, until mixture boils. Add chocolate mixture to sugar mixture; beat until smooth. Blend in buttermilk, baking soda, eggs and vanilla. Stir in marshmallows. Pour batter into prepared pan. Bake 40 to 45 minutes or until wooden pick inserted in center comes out clean. Meanwhile, prepare Chocolate Nut Frosting; spread over warm cake. Cool completely.

12 to 15 servings

*To sour milk: Use 1 1/2 teaspoons white vinegar plus milk to equal 1/2 cup.

Chocolate Nut Frosting

- 3 2/3 cups (1 pound) confectioners' sugar
- 1/2 cup butter or margarine
- 6 tablespoons cola (not diet)
- 3 tablespoons HERSHEY'S Cocoa
- 1/2 to 1 cup coarsely chopped pecans
- 1 teaspoon vanilla extract

In small mixer bowl place confectioners' sugar; set aside. In small saucepan combine butter, cola and cocoa. Cook over medium heat, stirring constantly, until mixture boils. Pour hot mixture over confectioners' sugar; beat until smooth and slightly thickened. Stir in pecans and vanilla.

About 2 1/2 cups frosting

Fudgey Pecan Torte

- 1 cup butter or margarine, melted
- 1 1/2 cups sugar
- 1 1/2 teaspoons vanilla extract
- 3 eggs, separated
- 2/3 cup HERSHEY'S Cocoa
- 1/2 cup all-purpose flour
- 3 tablespoons water
- 3/4 cup finely chopped pecans
- 1/8 teaspoon cream of tartar
- 1/8 teaspoon salt
- Royal Glaze (recipe follows)
- Pecan halves (optional)

Line bottom of 9-inch springform pan with aluminum foil; butter foil and side of pan. Heat oven to 350°. In large mixer bowl combine butter, sugar and vanilla; beat well. Add egg yolks, one at a time, beating well after each addition. Blend in cocoa, flour and water; beat well. Stir in chopped pecans. In small mixer bowl beat egg whites, cream of tartar and salt until stiff peaks form; carefully fold into chocolate mixture. Pour into prepared pan. Bake 45 minutes or until top begins to crack slightly. (Cake will not test done in center.) Cool 1 hour. Cover; chill until firm. Remove side of pan. Pour Royal Glaze over cake, allowing glaze to run down side. Spread glaze evenly on top and side. Allow to set. Garnish with pecan halves, if desired.

10 to 12 servings

Royal Glaze

In small saucepan combine 1 1/3 cups HERSHEY'S Semi-Sweet Chocolate Chips and 1/2 cup whipping cream. Cook over low heat, stirring constantly, until chips are melted and mixture begins to thicken.

Jubilee Chocolate Cake

- ¾ teaspoon baking soda
- 1 cup buttermilk or sour milk*
- 1½ cups cake flour or 1¼ cups all-purpose flour
- 1½ cups sugar, divided
- ½ cup HERSHEY'S Cocoa
- ½ teaspoon salt
- ½ cup vegetable oil
- 2 eggs, separated
- ½ teaspoon vanilla extract
- Vanilla ice cream
- Flaming Cherry Sauce (recipe follows)

In medium bowl stir baking soda into buttermilk until dissolved; set aside. Heat oven to 350°. Grease and flour 13×9×2-inch baking pan. In large mixer bowl combine flour, 1 cup sugar, cocoa and salt. Add oil, buttermilk mixture, egg yolks and vanilla; beat until smooth. In small mixer bowl beat egg whites until foamy; gradually add remaining ½ cup sugar, beating until stiff peaks form. Gently fold egg whites into chocolate batter. Pour batter into prepared pan. Bake 30 to 35 minutes or until cake springs back when touched lightly in center. Cool in pan on wire rack. Cut into squares; top each square with scoop of ice cream and serving of Flaming Cherry Sauce. *10 to 12 servings*

*To sour milk: Use 1 tablespoon white vinegar plus milk to equal 1 cup.

Flaming Cherry Sauce

- 1 can (16 or 17 ounces) pitted dark or light sweet cherries, drained (reserve ¾ cup liquid)
- 1½ tablespoons sugar
- 1 tablespoon cornstarch
- Dash salt
- ½ teaspoon grated orange peel
- ¼ cup kirsch or brandy

In saucepan or chafing dish stir together reserved cherry liquid, sugar, cornstarch and salt. Cook over medium heat, stirring constantly, until mixture boils; boil 1 minute. Add cherries and orange peel; heat thoroughly. In small saucepan over low heat gently heat kirsch or brandy; pour over cherry mixture. Carefully ignite with match. Stir gently; serve as directed. (Repeat procedure for sufficient amount of sauce for entire cake.)

4 to 6 servings

Black Forest Torte

Deep Dark Chocolate Cake (recipe page 18)
1 can (21 ounces) cherry pie filling, chilled
1 container (4 ounces) frozen whipped topping, thawed

Bake cake in two 9-inch round baking pans as directed. Cool 10 minutes; remove from pans. Cool completely. Place one layer on serving plate. Spoon half of pie filling in center and spread to within 1/2 inch of edge. Spoon or pipe border of whipped topping around edge. Top with second layer. Spoon remaining pie filling to within 1/2 inch of edge. Make border around top edge with remaining topping. Chill. *10 to 12 servings*

Triple Layer Chocolate Mousse Cake

Deep Dark Chocolate Cake (recipe page 18)
Chocolate Mousse, Double Recipe (recipe page 68)
Sliced almonds (optional)
Chocolate curls (optional)

Bake cake in three 8-inch round baking pans at 350° for 30 to 35 minutes. Cool 10 minutes; remove from pans. Cool completely. Prepare Chocolate Mousse, Double Recipe, according to directions. Fill and frost layers with mousse. Garnish with sliced almonds and chocolate curls, if desired. Chill at least 1 hour. Cover; refrigerate frosted cake.
10 to 12 servings

Cocoa Spice Snacking Cake

1/4 cup butter or margarine, melted
1/4 cup HERSHEY'S Cocoa
3/4 cup applesauce
1 cup all-purpose flour
1 cup granulated sugar
3/4 teaspoon baking soda
1/2 teaspoon ground cinnamon
1/4 teaspoon ground nutmeg
1/4 teaspoon salt
1 egg, slightly beaten
1/2 cup chopped nuts
1/2 cup raisins
Confectioners' sugar (optional)

Heat oven to 350°. Grease 9-inch square baking pan. In small bowl combine butter and cocoa, stirring until smooth; blend in applesauce. In large bowl combine flour, granulated sugar, baking soda, cinnamon, nutmeg and salt. Add cocoa mixture and egg; stir until dry ingredients are moistened. Stir in nuts and raisins. Spread into prepared pan; bake 30 to 35 minutes or until wooden pick inserted in center comes out clean. Cool in pan on wire rack. Cut into squares. Sprinkle confectioners' sugar over top, if desired. *9 servings*

Black Forest Torte (top) and Triple Layer Mousse Cake

Chocolate Swirl Cheesecake

- 4 packages (3 ounces each) cream cheese, softened
- 1/2 cup sugar
- 2 eggs
- 2 teaspoons vanilla extract
- 1/2 cup HERSHEY'S Semi-Sweet Chocolate Chips or MINI CHIPS Semi-Sweet Chocolate
- 1 teaspoon shortening
- 8-inch (6 ounces) packaged graham cracker crumb crust

Heat oven to 325°. In large mixer bowl beat cream cheese and sugar. Add eggs and vanilla; beat well. In small bowl reserve 1/2 cup cream cheese mixture. Melt chocolate chips with shortening in top of double boiler over hot, not boiling, water; stir into reserved 1/2 cup cream cheese mixture. Pour vanilla mixture into crust. Spoon chocolate mixture by dollops onto vanilla mixture. Using tip of knife swirl for marbled effect. Place filled crust on cookie sheet. Bake 25 to 30 minutes or until center is almost set. Cool. Cover; chill several hours or until firm. Garnish as desired.

8 servings

Elegant Peanut Butter Cheesecake

8-inch (6 ounces) packaged chocolate flavored crumb crust
1/4 cup HERSHEY'S Semi-Sweet Chocolate Chips
2 cups (12-ounce package) REESE'S Peanut Butter Chips
1 package (8 ounces) cream cheese, softened
1/2 cup packed light brown sugar
3 egg yolks
1 cup chilled whipping cream
3/4 cup chopped unsalted, roasted peanuts, divided

Heat oven to 350°. Heat crust in oven 5 minutes. Remove from oven; sprinkle chocolate chips in bottom of crust. When chips melt, spread over bottom of crust. Chill crust 5 to 10 minutes or until chocolate hardens. In top of double boiler over hot, not boiling, water melt peanut butter chips, stirring constantly to blend; cool slightly. In large mixer bowl beat cream cheese, melted peanut butter chips, brown sugar and egg yolks until smooth. In small mixer bowl beat whipping cream until stiff. Fold whipped cream and 1/2 cup peanuts into cream cheese mixture; spoon into crust. Sprinkle remaining 1/4 cup peanuts over top. Cover; chill until firm. Garnish as desired.

8 servings

From left to right: Easy Peanut Butter Chocolate Chip Cake, Double Marble Cake and Double Chocolate Snack Cake

Easy Peanut Butter-Chocolate Chip Cake

- 1 package (18.5 ounces) yellow cake mix (with pudding in the mix)
- 4 eggs
- 3/4 cup water
- 1/3 cup vegetable oil
- 1/3 cup creamy peanut butter
- 1 1/2 cups HERSHEY'S Semi-Sweet Chocolate Chips, divided
- 1/4 cup chopped, unsalted peanuts

Heat oven to 350°. Grease and lightly flour 13×9×2-inch baking pan. Prepare cake batter according to package directions using eggs, water and oil. Blend in peanut butter. Spoon half of batter into prepared pan. Sprinkle 3/4 cup chocolate chips over batter. Gently spread remaining batter over top. Sprinkle remaining 3/4 cup chips and peanuts over batter. Bake 45 minutes or until wooden pick inserted in center comes out clean. Cool in pan on wire rack.

12 to 15 servings

Double Marble Cake

- 1 package (18.25 or 19.75 ounces) fudge marble cake mix
- 3 eggs
- 1/3 cup vegetable oil
- Water
- 1 cup HERSHEY'S Semi-Sweet Chocolate Chips, divided
- 1 jar (7 ounces) marshmallow creme

Heat oven to 350°. Grease and flour 13×9×2-inch baking pan. Prepare cake batters according to package directions, using eggs, oil and water. Stir 1/2 cup chocolate chips into chocolate batter. Spoon vanilla and chocolate batters into prepared pan; swirl as directed on package. Bake 33 to 38 minutes or until wooden pick inserted in center comes out clean. Cool in pan on wire rack 5 minutes. Gently spread marshmallow creme over warm cake. In small saucepan over low heat melt remaining 1/2 cup chips; swirl through marshmallow creme. Cool thoroughly.

12 to 15 servings

Double Chocolate Snack Cake

- 1 2/3 cups all-purpose flour
- 1 cup packed light brown sugar
- 1/4 cup HERSHEY'S Cocoa
- 1 teaspoon baking soda
- 1/4 teaspoon salt
- 1 cup water
- 1/3 cup vegetable oil
- 1 teaspoon white vinegar
- 3/4 teaspoon vanilla extract
- 1/2 cup HERSHEY'S Semi-Sweet Chocolate Chips

Heat oven to 350°. Grease and flour 8-inch square baking pan. In small bowl combine flour, sugar, cocoa, baking soda and salt. Add water, oil, vinegar and vanilla; beat with spoon or wire whisk until smooth. Pour batter into prepared pan. Sprinkle chocolate chips over top. Bake 35 to 40 minutes or until wooden pick inserted in center comes out clean. Cool in pan on wire rack.

6 to 8 servings

VARIATION

Chocolate Banana Snack Cake: Decrease water to 1/2 cup; stir in 1/2 cup mashed, ripe banana (1 medium banana) before pouring batter into pan.

Chocolate Raisin Snacking Cake

- 3/4 cup raisins
- 1 cup water
- 1 1/4 cups granulated sugar
- 2/3 cup vegetable oil
- 1 egg, slightly beaten
- 1 3/4 cups all-purpose flour
- 1/3 cup HERSHEY'S Cocoa
- 1 teaspoon baking soda
- 1/2 teaspoon salt
- 1/4 teaspoon ground cinnamon
- 1/2 cup chopped nuts
- Confectioners' sugar

Heat oven to 350°. Grease and flour 13 x 9 x 2-inch baking pan. In medium saucepan bring raisins and water to boil; simmer 1 minute. Remove from heat; cool slightly. Stir in granulated sugar and oil. Add egg. Combine flour, cocoa, baking soda, salt and cinnamon; stir into raisin mixture, blending well. Stir in nuts. Pour batter into prepared pan. Bake 25 to 30 minutes or until wooden pick inserted in center comes out clean. Sprinkle confectioners' sugar over warm cake. Cool in pan on wire rack.

12 to 15 servings

Cocoa Marble Gingerbread

- 1/2 cup shortening
- 1 cup sugar
- 1 cup light molasses
- 2 eggs
- 1 teaspoon baking soda
- 1 cup boiling water
- 2 cups all-purpose flour
- 1 teaspoon salt
- 1/4 cup HERSHEY'S Cocoa
- 1/2 teaspoon ground cinnamon
- 1/2 teaspoon ground ginger
- 1/4 teaspoon ground nutmeg
- 1/4 teaspoon ground cloves
- Sweetened whipped cream (optional)

Heat oven to 350°. Grease and flour 13 x 9 x 2-inch baking pan. In large mixer bowl combine shortening, sugar and molasses; beat well. Blend in eggs. Stir baking soda into boiling water, stirring to dissolve; add alternately with flour and salt to creamed mixture. In medium bowl stir cocoa into 2 cups batter. Add spices to remaining batter in large mixer bowl. Alternately spoon batters into prepared pan. Swirl gently with metal spatula or knife to marble. Bake 40 to 45 minutes or until wooden pick inserted in center comes out clean. Cut into squares. Serve warm or cool with sweetened whipped cream, if desired.

12 servings

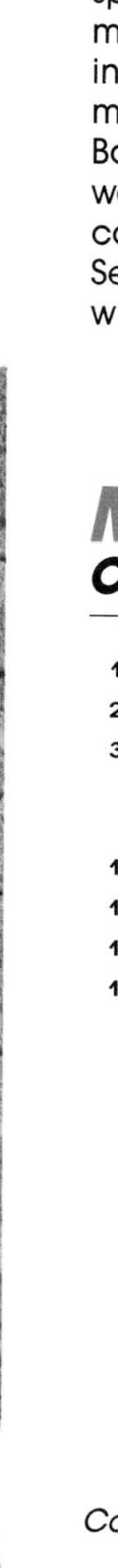

Microwave Chocolate Cake

- 1/4 cup HERSHEY'S Cocoa
- 2/3 cup hot water, divided
- 3/4 cup plus 2 tablespoons all-purpose flour
- 1 cup sugar
- 1/2 teaspoon baking soda
- 1/4 teaspoon baking powder
- 1/4 teaspoon salt
- 1/4 cup plus 2 tablespoons vegetable oil
- 1 egg
- 2 teaspoons vanilla extract
- Easy Cocoa Frosting (recipe follows)

Cocoa Marble Gingerbread

Microwave Chocolate Cake

Grease microwave-safe 7¼ × 2¼-inch or 8 × 1½-inch round baking dish. Line bottom of dish with plastic wrap. In small microwave-safe bowl combine cocoa and ⅓ cup water; microwave at HIGH (100%) 40 to 50 seconds or until very hot and slightly thickened. In medium bowl combine flour, sugar, baking soda, baking powder and salt. Add oil, remaining ⅓ cup hot water, egg, vanilla and chocolate mixture; beat with whisk 40 to 50 strokes or until batter is smooth and well blended. Pour batter into prepared pan. Microwave at HIGH 5 to 6 minutes*, without turning, until cake begins to pull away from sides (some moist spots may remain but will disappear on standing). Let stand 5 minutes; invert onto serving plate. Peel off plastic wrap; cool. Frost with Easy Cocoa Frosting. Garnish as desired.

About 8 servings

*Time is for 600-700 watt microwave ovens. Increase baking time for lower wattage ovens.

Easy Cocoa Frosting

3 tablespoons butter or margarine, softened
¼ cup HERSHEY'S Cocoa
1⅓ cups confectioners' sugar
2 to 3 tablespoons milk
½ teaspoon vanilla extract

In small mixer bowl combine all ingredients; beat to spreading consistency. *About 1 cup frosting.*

Individual Cocoa Cheesecakes

- $^1/_3$ cup graham cracker crumbs
- $^1/_3$ cup plus 1 tablespoon sugar, divided
- 1 tablespoon butter or margarine, melted
- 1 package (8 ounces) cream cheese, softened
- 3 tablespoons HERSHEY'S Cocoa
- 1 teaspoon vanilla extract
- 1 tablespoon milk
- 1 egg

Microwave Directions: In small bowl combine graham cracker crumbs, 1 tablespoon sugar and butter. Press about 1 tablespoon crumb mixture onto bottom of 6 microwave-safe ramekins ($2^1/_2$ to 3 inches in diameter). In small mixer bowl beat cream cheese, remaining $^1/_3$ cup sugar, cocoa and vanilla. Add milk and egg, beating just until smooth and well blended. Divide mixture evenly among ramekins, filling each to $^1/_4$ inch from top. Microwave at MEDIUM-HIGH (70%) 2 minutes, rotating dishes after 1 minute. Microwave at HIGH (100%) 30 to 40 seconds or until puffed in center. Cool; chill before serving. Garnish as desired. *6 cheesecakes*

Note: Substitute paper-lined microwave-safe muffin cups ($2^1/_2$ inches in diameter) for ramekins, if desired.

From top to bottom: Simple Chocolate Cheesecakes, Black-Eyed Susan Cheesecakes (recipes page 34) and Individual Cocoa Cheesecakes

Simple Chocolate Cheesecakes

24 vanilla wafer cookies
2 packages (8 ounces each) cream cheese, softened
1 1/4 cups sugar
1/3 cup HERSHEY'S Cocoa
2 tablespoons all-purpose flour
3 eggs
1 cup dairy sour cream
1 teaspoon vanilla extract
Sour Cream Topping (recipe follows)
Canned cherry pie filling, chilled

Heat oven to 350°. Line muffin pans with foil-laminated paper bake cups (2 1/2 inches in diameter). Place one vanilla wafer in bottom of each cup. In large mixer bowl beat cream cheese and sugar. Blend in cocoa and flour. Add eggs; beat well. Blend in sour cream and vanilla. Fill each prepared cup almost full with cheese mixture. Bake 15 to 20 minutes or just until set. Remove from oven; cool 5 to 10 minutes. Spread heaping teaspoonful Sour Cream Topping on surface of each cup. Cool completely; chill. Garnish with cherry pie filling just before serving.

About 2 dozen cheesecakes

Sour Cream Topping

In small bowl combine 1 cup dairy sour cream, 2 tablespoons sugar and 1 teaspoon vanilla extract; stir until sugar dissolves.

Black-Eyed Susan Cheesecakes

24 vanilla wafer cookies
2 packages (8 ounces each) cream cheese, softened
1/2 cup sugar
2 eggs
1/2 teaspoon vanilla extract
1 cup REESE'S Peanut Butter Chips
1/2 cup HERSHEY'S Semi-Sweet Chocolate Chips
3 tablespoons butter or margarine

Heat oven to 350°. Line muffin pans with foil-laminated paper bake cups (2 inches in diameter). Place one vanilla wafer in bottom of each cup. In large mixer bowl beat cream cheese and sugar. Add eggs and vanilla; beat well. Stir in peanut butter chips. Spoon 1 heaping tablespoon cheese mixture into each cup. Bake 15 minutes or just until set, but not browned. Cool. In small microwave-safe bowl place chocolate chips and butter. Microwave at HIGH (100%) 30 seconds to 1 minute or until chips are melted and mixture is smooth when stirred. Drop teaspoonfuls of chocolate mixture onto center of each cheesecake, letting white show around edge. Garnish as desired. Cover; chill.

About 2 dozen cheesecakes

Banana Chip Bundt Cake

- 1 package (18.5 ounces) banana cake mix (with pudding in the mix)
- 1 package ($3\frac{1}{2}$ ounces) instant banana cream pudding and pie filling
- 4 eggs
- 1 cup water
- $\frac{1}{2}$ cup vegetable oil
- 1 cup HERSHEY'S MINI CHIPS Semi-Sweet Chocolate
- Chocolate Glaze (recipe follows)

Heat oven to 350°. Grease and flour 12-cup Bundt pan. In large mixer bowl combine cake mix, pudding mix, eggs, water and oil; beat on low speed just until blended. Increase speed to medium; beat 2 minutes. Stir in MINI CHIPS Chocolate. Pour batter into prepared pan. Bake 45 to 50 minutes or until wooden pick inserted in center comes out clean. Cool 10 minutes; remove from pan. Cool completely on wire rack. Drizzle with Chocolate Glaze.

12 to 16 servings

Chocolate Glaze

In small saucepan bring $\frac{1}{3}$ cup sugar and $\frac{1}{4}$ cup water to full boil, stirring until sugar dissolves. Remove from heat; add 1 cup HERSHEY'S MINI CHIPS Semi-Sweet Chocolate. Stir with wire whisk until chips are melted and mixture is smooth. Cool to desired consistency; use immediately.

About $\frac{2}{3}$ cup glaze

Aztec Sunburst Cake

- ¾ cup plus 2 tablespoons butter or margarine, divided
- ½ cup packed light brown sugar
- 2 tablespoons light corn syrup
- 1 can (16 ounces) pear halves (4 to 6 halves)
- 7 maraschino cherries, cut into quarters
- ½ cup pecan halves
- 1¼ cups granulated sugar
- 1 teaspoon vanilla extract
- 2 eggs
- 1½ cups all-purpose flour
- ¼ cup HERSHEY'S Cocoa
- ½ teaspoon baking soda
- ½ teaspoon salt
- ½ cup buttermilk or sour milk*
- Sweetened whipped cream (optional)

Heat oven to 350°. In 9-inch square baking pan melt ¼ cup butter in oven. Stir in brown sugar and corn syrup; spread evenly in pan. Drain pear halves; slice each half lengthwise into 4 sections, if desired, and place in sunburst design over mixture in pan. Arrange cherries and pecans between pear sections, in center and at corners. In large mixer bowl cream remaining ½ cup plus 2 tablespoons butter, granulated sugar and vanilla. Add eggs; beat well. Combine flour, cocoa, baking soda and salt; add alternately with buttermilk to creamed mixture. Carefully pour batter over fruit and nuts in pan. Bake 50 to 55 minutes or until wooden pick inserted in center comes out clean. Immediately invert onto serving plate. Serve warm or cold with sweetened whipped cream, if desired.

8 to 10 servings

*To sour milk: Use 1½ teaspoons white vinegar plus milk to equal ½ cup.

Cocoa Chiffon Cake

2 cups sugar, divided
1 1/2 cups cake flour
2/3 cup HERSHEY'S Cocoa
2 teaspoons baking powder
1 teaspoon salt
1/2 teaspoon baking soda
1/2 cup vegetable oil
7 eggs, separated
3/4 cup cold water
2 teaspoons vanilla extract
1/2 teaspoon cream of tartar
Vanilla Glaze (recipe follows)

Heat oven to 325°. In large bowl combine 1 3/4 cups sugar, flour, cocoa, baking powder, salt and baking soda. Add oil, egg yolks, water and vanilla; beat until smooth. In large mixer bowl beat egg whites and cream of tartar until foamy. Gradually add remaining 1/4 cup sugar, beating until stiff peaks form. Gradually pour chocolate batter over beaten egg whites, folding with rubber spatula just until blended. Pour into ungreased 10-inch tube pan. Bake 1 hour and 20 minutes or until top springs back when touched lightly. Invert pan on heatproof funnel until completely cool. Remove cake from pan; invert onto serving plate. Spread top of cake with Vanilla Glaze, allowing some to drizzle down side. *12 to 16 servings*

Vanilla Glaze

1/3 cup butter or margarine
2 cups confectioners' sugar
1 1/2 teaspoons vanilla extract
2 to 4 tablespoons hot water

In medium saucepan over low heat melt butter. Remove from heat. Stir in confectioners' sugar and vanilla. Stir in water, 1 tablespoon at a time, until smooth and of desired consistency.
About 1 1/4 cups glaze

German Chocolate Cake

- 1/4 cup HERSHEY'S Cocoa
- 1/2 cup boiling water
- 1 cup plus 3 tablespoons butter or margarine
- 2 1/4 cups sugar
- 1 teaspoon vanilla extract
- 4 eggs
- 2 cups all-purpose flour
- 1 teaspoon baking soda
- 1/2 teaspoon salt
- 1 cup buttermilk or sour milk*
- Coconut Pecan Frosting (recipe follows)
- Pecan halves (optional)

In small bowl combine cocoa and water; stir until smooth. Set aside to cool. Heat oven to 350°. Grease three 9-inch round baking pans; line bottoms with wax paper. In large mixer bowl cream butter. Add sugar and vanilla; beat until light and fluffy. Add eggs, one at a time, beating well after each addition. Combine flour, baking soda and salt; add alternately with chocolate mixture and buttermilk to creamed mixture. Mix only until smooth. Pour batter into prepared pans. Bake 25 to 30 minutes or until top springs back when touched lightly in center. Cool 5 minutes; remove from pans and peel off paper. Cool completely. Spread Coconut Pecan Frosting between layers and over top. Garnish with pecan halves, if desired. Cover; refrigerate frosted cake.

10 to 12 servings

*To sour milk: Use 1 tablespoon white vinegar plus milk to equal 1 cup.

Coconut Pecan Frosting

- 1 can (14 ounces) sweetened condensed milk
- 3 egg yolks, beaten
- 1/2 cup butter or margarine
- 1 teaspoon vanilla extract
- 1 can (3 1/2 ounces) flaked coconut (about 1 1/3 cups)
- 1 cup chopped pecans

In heavy 2-quart saucepan combine sweetened condensed milk, egg yolks and butter. Cook, stirring constantly, over medium heat until mixture is thickened and bubbly, about 10 minutes. Remove from heat; stir in vanilla, coconut and pecans. Cool about 15 minutes.

About 2 3/4 cups frosting

Apple-Chip Snacking Cake

- 2 eggs
- 1/2 cup vegetable oil
- 1/4 cup bottled apple juice
- 1 teaspoon vanilla extract
- 1 3/4 cups all-purpose flour
- 1 cup sugar
- 1/2 teaspoon baking soda
- 1/2 teaspoon ground cinnamon
- 1/2 teaspoon salt
- 1 1/2 cups diced peeled tart apples
- 3/4 cup HERSHEY'S Semi-Sweet Chocolate Chips or MINI CHIPS
- 1/2 cup chopped nuts
- Whipped topping and cinnamon

Heat oven to 350°. Grease and flour 9-inch square baking pan. In large bowl beat eggs slightly; gradually blend in oil, apple juice and vanilla. Combine flour, sugar, baking soda, cinnamon and salt; stir into batter until combined. Add apples, chocolate chips and nuts; stir until well blended. Pour into prepared pan. Bake 40 to 45 minutes or until cake begins to pull away from sides of pan. Cool completely. Serve with dollop of whipped topping sprinkled with cinnamon. Garnish as desired.

9 servings

Cocoa Oatmeal Cake

- 1 1/3 cups boiling water
- 1 cup quick-cooking rolled oats
- 1/2 cup butter or margarine, softened
- 1 cup granulated sugar
- 1 cup packed light brown sugar
- 2 eggs
- 1 1/2 cups all-purpose flour
- 1/2 cup HERSHEY'S Cocoa
- 1 teaspoon baking powder
- 1 teaspoon baking soda
- 1/4 teaspoon ground cinnamon
- 1 cup finely chopped, peeled apple
- 1 cup chopped nuts
- Vanilla Glaze (recipe follows)

In small bowl pour boiling water over oats; let stand 15 minutes. Heat oven to 350°. Grease and flour 13 × 9 × 2-inch baking pan. In large mixer bowl cream butter, granulated sugar, brown sugar and eggs until light and fluffy. Blend in oat mixture. Combine flour, cocoa, baking powder, baking soda and cinnamon; add to creamed mixture, mixing well. Stir in apple and nuts. Pour batter into prepared pan. Bake 30 to 35 minutes or until wooden pick inserted in center comes out clean. Cool in pan on wire rack; drizzle Vanilla Glaze over top in decorative design.

12 to 15 servings

Vanilla Glaze

- 1 cup confectioners' sugar
- 1 tablespoon butter or margarine, softened
- 1 to 2 tablespoons hot water
- 1/2 teaspoon vanilla extract

In small bowl beat all ingredients with spoon or wire whisk until smooth.

Chocolate Chip Orange Pound Cake

- 1/2 cup butter, softened
- 4 ounces (1/2 of 8-ounce package) cream cheese, softened
- 3/4 cup sugar
- 2 eggs
- 1 teaspoon vanilla extract
- 1/4 teaspoon grated orange peel
- 1 cup all-purpose flour
- 1 teaspoon baking powder
- 1 cup HERSHEY'S MINI CHIPS Semi-Sweet Chocolate
- Confectioners' sugar

Heat oven to 325°. Grease and flour 9 x 5 x 3-inch loaf pan. Cut butter and cream cheese into 1-inch slices; place in bowl of food processor. Add sugar; process until smooth, about 30 seconds. Add eggs, vanilla and orange peel; process until blended, about 10 seconds. Add flour and baking powder; process until blended, about 10 seconds. Stir in MINI CHIPS Chocolate. Pour batter into prepared pan. Bake 45 to 50 minutes or until cake pulls away from sides of pan. Cool 10 minutes; remove from pan. Cool completely on wire rack. Sprinkle confectioners' sugar over cake.

About 10 servings

Cocoa Cheesecake

Graham Crust (recipe follows)
2 packages (8 ounces each) cream cheese, softened
3/4 cup plus 2 tablespoons sugar, divided
1/2 cup HERSHEY'S Cocoa
2 teaspoons vanilla extract, divided
2 eggs
1 cup dairy sour cream

Prepare Graham Crust; set aside. Heat oven to 375°. In large mixer bowl beat cream cheese, 3/4 cup sugar, cocoa and 1 teaspoon vanilla until light and fluffy. Add eggs; blend well. Pour batter into prepared crust. Bake 20 minutes. Remove from oven; cool 15 minutes. Increase oven temperature to 425°. In small bowl combine sour cream, remaining 2 tablespoons sugar and remaining 1 teaspoon vanilla; stir until smooth. Spread evenly over baked filling. Bake 10 minutes. Cool; chill several hours or overnight.

10 to 12 servings

Graham Crust

In small bowl combine 1 1/2 cups graham cracker crumbs, 1/3 cup sugar and 1/3 cup melted butter or margarine. Press mixture onto bottom and halfway up side of 9-inch springform pan.

Chocolate Lover's Cheesecake: Prepare as above, adding 1 cup HERSHEY'S Semi-Sweet Chocolate Chips after eggs have been blended into mixture. Bake and serve as directed.

Cocoa Cheesecake

Chocolate Buttermilk Cake

1 2/3 cups all-purpose flour
1 1/2 cups sugar
2/3 cup HERSHEY'S Cocoa
1 1/2 teaspoons baking soda
1 teaspoon salt
1/2 cup shortening
1 1/2 cups buttermilk or sour milk*
1 teaspoon vanilla extract
2 eggs
Jiffy Chocolate Frosting (recipe follows)

Heat oven to 350°. Grease and flour 13 x 9 x 2-inch baking pan. In large mixer bowl combine all ingredients except Jiffy Chocolate Frosting. Blend on low speed 30 seconds, scraping bottom and sides of bowl constantly. Beat 3 minutes on medium speed, scraping bowl occasionally. Pour batter into prepared pan. Bake 35 to 40 minutes or until wooden pick inserted in center comes out clean. Cool in pan on wire rack. Frost with Jiffy Chocolate Frosting.

12 to 15 servings

*To sour milk: Use 1 tablespoon plus 1 1/2 teaspoons white vinegar plus milk to equal 1 1/2 cups.

Jiffy Chocolate Frosting

1 cup HERSHEY'S Semi-Sweet Chocolate Chips
1 cup confectioners' sugar
1/3 cup evaporated milk

In small microwave-safe bowl place chocolate chips. Microwave at HIGH (100%) 1 minute; stir. Microwave at HIGH additional 30 seconds or until melted and smooth when stirred. Gradually add confectioners' sugar and evaporated milk, beating until smooth.

About 1 1/4 cups frosting

Mississippi Mud Cake

- 1/2 cup butter or margarine
- 1 cup sugar
- 1 teaspoon vanilla extract
- 3 eggs
- 3/4 cup all-purpose flour
- 1/3 cup HERSHEY'S Cocoa
- 1/2 teaspoon baking powder
- Dash salt
- 1 cup chopped pecans
- 1 package (10 1/2 ounces) miniature marshmallows
- One-Bowl Buttercream Frosting (recipe page 191)

Heat oven to 350°. Grease 13×9×2-inch baking pan. In large mixer bowl cream butter, sugar and vanilla until light and fluffy. Add eggs, one at a time, beating well after each addition. Combine flour, cocoa, baking powder and salt; add to creamed mixture. Stir in pecans. Spoon batter into prepared pan. Bake 15 to 18 minutes or until top is barely soft to the touch. Meanwhile, prepare frosting. Remove cake from oven; immediately place marshmallows over top. Return cake to oven 2 to 3 minutes or until marshmallows are soft. Gently spread marshmallows over cake; immediately spread frosting over top. Cool thoroughly on wire rack before cutting cake into squares.

12 to 15 servings

Chocolate Cherry Upside-Down Cake

- 1 tablespoon cold water
- 1 tablespoon cornstarch
- 1/4 to 1/2 teaspoon almond extract (optional)
- 1 can (21 ounces) cherry pie filling
- 1 2/3 cups all-purpose flour
- 1 cup sugar
- 1/4 cup HERSHEY'S Cocoa
- 1 teaspoon baking soda
- 1/2 teaspoon salt
- 1 cup water
- 1/3 cup vegetable oil
- 1 teaspoon white vinegar
- 1/2 teaspoon vanilla extract

Heat oven to 350°. In medium bowl combine cold water, cornstarch and almond extract, if desired. Stir in cherry pie filling; blend well. Spread evenly on bottom of ungreased 9-inch square baking pan; set aside. In medium bowl combine flour, sugar, cocoa, baking soda and salt. Add water, oil, vinegar and vanilla; beat with spoon or wire whisk until batter is smooth and well blended. Pour evenly over cherries. Bake 40 to 45 minutes or until wooden pick inserted in center comes out clean. Cool 10 minutes; invert onto serving plate. Serve warm.

About 9 servings

Ice Cream Cake

- 3 cups ice cream, softened
- Deep Dark Chocolate Cake (recipe page 18)
- One-Bowl Buttercream Frosting (recipe page 191) OR
- 1 container (8 ounces) frozen whipped topping, thawed

Line 9-inch round pan with aluminum foil. Firmly pack ice cream into pan. Cover; freeze about 3 hours. Bake cake in two 9-inch round baking pans as directed. Cool 10 minutes; remove from pans. Cool completely. Place one cake layer upside down on serving plate. Unmold ice cream layer from pan on top of cake layer; peel off foil. Place second cake layer, top side up, over ice cream layer. Gently spread One-Bowl Buttercream Frosting or whipped topping on top and side of cake. Cover and freeze at least 1 hour before serving. Garnish as desired.

10 to 12 servings

Hershey's Chocolate Fudge Cake

- 3/4 cup butter or margarine
- 1 2/3 cups sugar
- 3 eggs
- 1 1/2 teaspoons vanilla extract
- 2 cups all-purpose flour
- 2/3 cup HERSHEY'S Cocoa
- 1 1/4 teaspoons baking soda
- 1/2 teaspoon baking powder
- 1/2 teaspoon salt
- 1 1/3 cups milk
- Chocolate Fudge Frosting (recipe follows)

Heat oven to 350°. Grease and flour two 9-inch round baking pans or 13 x 9 x 2-inch baking pan. In large mixer bowl cream butter; gradually add sugar and continue beating until light and fluffy. Add eggs, one at a time, beating well after each addition. Blend in vanilla. Beat at medium speed 5 minutes, scraping sides of bowl occasionally. Combine flour, cocoa, baking soda, baking powder and salt; add to creamed mixture alternately with milk, beginning and ending with dry ingredients and beating just enough to blend. Pour batter into prepared pan(s). Bake 35 to 40 minutes or until wooden pick inserted in center comes out clean. Cool cake in rounds 10 minutes on wire rack. Remove from pans; cool completely. (Cake may be left in rectangular pan, if desired.) Frost with Chocolate Fudge Frosting. Garnish as desired.

8 to 10 servings

Chocolate Fudge Frosting*

3/4 cup butter or margarine
1 cup HERSHEY'S Cocoa
4 cups confectioners' sugar
1/2 cup hot milk
2 teaspoons vanilla extract

In small saucepan over low heat melt butter; add cocoa, stirring constantly until smooth and slightly thickened. Remove from heat; set aside to cool slightly. In large mixer bowl combine confectioners' sugar and milk; beat until smooth. Add chocolate mixture and vanilla. Beat on medium speed until smooth and slightly thickened, 5 to 10 minutes. Cool at room temperature to spreading consistency, about 1/2 hour.

About 3 cups frosting

*For 13 × 9 × 2-inch cake use 6 tablespoons butter or margarine, 1/2 cup cocoa, 2 cups confectioners' sugar, 1/4 cup hot milk and 1 teaspoon vanilla extract; follow directions above for preparation.

About 1 1/2 cups frosting

Chocolate Stripe Cake

- **1 package (18.25 ounces) white cake mix**
- **1 envelope unflavored gelatin**
- **1/4 cup cold water**
- **1/4 cup boiling water**
- **1 cup HERSHEY'S Syrup**
- **Whipped topping**
- **HERSHEY'S Syrup (optional garnish)**

Heat oven to 350°. Grease and flour 13 x 9 x 2-inch baking pan. Prepare cake batter and bake according to package directions. Cool 15 minutes. Do not remove cake from pan. With fork, carefully pierce cake to bottom of pan, making rows about 1 inch apart covering length and width of cake. In small bowl sprinkle gelatin over cold water; let stand 1 minute to soften. Add boiling water; stir until gelatin is completely dissolved and mixture is clear. Stir in 1 cup syrup. Pour chocolate mixture evenly over cooled cake, making sure entire top is covered and mixture has flowed into holes. Cover; chill about 5 hours or until set. Serve with whipped topping; garnish with syrup, if desired. Refrigerate leftovers.

12 to 15 servings

Cream Filled Banana Cupcakes

- **Cream Cheese Filling (recipe follows)**
- **1 package (18.5 ounces) banana cake mix (with pudding in the mix)**
- **3/4 cup finely chopped nuts**
- **2 tablespoons sugar**

Prepare Cream Cheese Filling; set aside. Heat oven to 350°. Prepare cake batter according to package directions. Fill paper-lined muffin cups (2 1/2 inches in diameter) 1/2 full with batter. Spoon about 1 teaspoonful filling into center of each cupcake. Combine nuts and sugar; sprinkle about 1 teaspoonful over top of each cupcake. Bake 20 minutes or until wooden pick inserted in cake portion comes out clean. Cool on wire rack.

About 3 dozen cupcakes

Cream Cheese Filling

- **1 package (8 ounces) cream cheese, softened**
- **1/3 cup sugar**
- **1 egg**
- **1 cup HERSHEY'S MINI CHIPS Semi-Sweet Chocolate**

In small mixer bowl combine cream cheese, sugar and egg; beat until smooth. Stir in MINI CHIPS Chocolate.

Chocolate Stripe Cake (top) and Cream Filled Banana Cupcakes

Old-Fashioned Chocolate Cake

- 3/4 cup butter or margarine
- 1 2/3 cups sugar
- 3 eggs
- 1 teaspoon vanilla extract
- 2 cups all-purpose flour
- 2/3 cup HERSHEY'S Cocoa
- 1 1/4 teaspoons baking soda
- 1/4 teaspoon baking powder
- 1 teaspoon salt
- 1 1/3 cups water
- 1/2 cup finely crushed hard peppermint candy (optional)
- One-Bowl Buttercream Frosting (recipe page 191)
- Additional crushed peppermint candy (optional)

Heat oven to 350°. Grease and flour two 9-inch round baking pans or 13 x 9 x 2-inch baking pan. In large mixer bowl combine butter, sugar, eggs and vanilla. Beat on high speed 3 minutes. Combine flour, cocoa, baking soda, baking powder and salt; add alternately with water to creamed mixture. Blend just until combined. Add candy, if desired. Pour into prepared pan(s). Bake 30 to 35 minutes or until wooden pick inserted in center comes out clean. Cool 10 minutes; remove from pan(s) to wire rack. Cool completely. Frost with One-Bowl Buttercream Frosting. Garnish with additional candy, if desired. *8 to 10 servings*

Chocolate Cupcakes: Heat oven to 350°. Fill paper-lined muffin cups (2 1/2 inches in diameter) 2/3 full with batter. Bake 20 to 25 minutes. Cool and frost.

About 2 1/2 dozen cupcakes

Mocha Cheesecake

Chocolate Cookie Crust (recipe follows)
4 packages (3 ounces each) cream cheese, softened
2½ tablespoons butter or margarine, softened
1 cup sugar
2 eggs
5 tablespoons HERSHEY'S Cocoa
¾ teaspoon vanilla extract
1 tablespoon powdered instant coffee
1 teaspoon boiling water
1 cup dairy sour cream

Prepare Chocolate Cookie Crust; set aside. Heat oven to 325°. In large mixer bowl beat cream cheese and butter until smooth and fluffy. Gradually beat in sugar. Add eggs, one at a time, beating well after each addition. Beat in cocoa and vanilla. Dissolve instant coffee in water; stir into cheese mixture. Add sour cream; blend well. Pour mixture into pan. Bake 30 minutes. Turn off oven; leave cheesecake in oven 15 minutes without opening door. Remove from oven. Cool in pan on wire rack. Cover; chill. Garnish as desired.

10 to 12 servings

Chocolate Cookie Crust

22 chocolate wafers (½ of 8½-ounce package)
¼ cup cold butter or margarine, cut into ½-inch slices
⅛ teaspoon ground cinnamon

Crush wafers in food processor or blender to form fine crumbs. In medium bowl mix crumbs, butter and cinnamon until evenly blended. Press mixture evenly on bottom of 9-inch springform pan.

Mocha Fudge Pudding Cake

- 1 cup all-purpose biscuit baking mix
- 1 cup granulated sugar, divided
- 7 tablespoons HERSHEY'S Cocoa, divided
- 1/2 cup milk
- 1 teaspoon vanilla extract
- 1/4 cup packed light brown sugar
- 1 cup hot coffee
- 1/2 cup hot water
- Whipped topping

Heat oven to 350°. In medium bowl combine baking mix, 3/4 cup granulated sugar and 3 tablespoons cocoa. Add milk and vanilla; beat with spoon until well blended. Spoon into 8-inch square baking pan. In small bowl combine remaining 1/4 cup granulated sugar, remaining 4 tablespoons cocoa and brown sugar; sprinkle evenly over batter. Pour coffee and water over top; *do not stir.* Bake 40 minutes or until top is firm. Cool 15 minutes. Spoon into dessert dishes, spooning sauce from bottom of pan over top. Serve immediately with whipped topping.

6 to 8 servings

Cocoa Bundt Cake

- 1 2/3 cups all-purpose flour
- 1 1/2 cups sugar
- 1/2 cup HERSHEY'S Cocoa
- 1 1/2 teaspoons baking soda
- 1 teaspoon salt
- 1/2 teaspoon baking powder
- 2 eggs
- 1/2 cup shortening
- 1 1/2 cups buttermilk or sour milk*
- 1 teaspoon vanilla extract
- Cocoa Glaze (recipe follows)

Heat oven to 350°. Generously grease and flour 12-cup Bundt pan. In large mixer bowl blend flour, sugar, cocoa, baking soda, salt and baking powder; add remaining ingredients except Cocoa Glaze. Beat on low speed 1 minute, scraping bowl constantly. Beat on high speed 3 minutes, scraping bowl occasionally. Pour into prepared pan. Bake 50 to 55 minutes or until wooden pick inserted in center comes out clean. Cool 10 minutes; remove from pan to wire rack. Cool completely. Drizzle with Cocoa Glaze.

12 to 16 servings

*To sour milk: Use 1 tablespoon plus 1 1/2 teaspoons white vinegar plus milk to equal 1 1/2 cups.

Cocoa Glaze

- 2 tablespoons butter or margarine
- 2 tablespoons HERSHEY'S Cocoa
- 2 tablespoons water
- 1 cup confectioners' sugar
- 1/2 teaspoon vanilla extract

In small saucepan over low heat melt butter; add cocoa and water, stirring constantly, until mixture thickens. *Do not boil.* Remove from heat; gradually add confectioners' sugar and vanilla, beating with wire whisk until smooth. Add additional water, 1/2 teaspoon at a time, until desired consistency.

About 3/4 cup glaze

VARIATION

Cocoa Sheet Cake: Prepare batter as directed; pour into greased and floured 13 x 9 x 2-inch baking pan. Bake at 350° for 35 to 40 minutes or until wooden pick inserted in center comes out clean. Cool completely; frost with One-Bowl Buttercream Frosting (recipe page 191).

Cocoa Bundt Cake

Black Magic Cake

- $1\frac{3}{4}$ cups all-purpose flour
- 2 cups sugar
- $\frac{3}{4}$ cup HERSHEY'S Cocoa
- 2 teaspoons baking soda
- 1 teaspoon baking powder
- 1 teaspoon salt
- 2 eggs
- 1 cup strong black coffee (or 2 teaspoons powdered instant coffee plus 1 cup boiling water)
- 1 cup buttermilk or sour milk*
- $\frac{1}{2}$ cup vegetable oil
- 1 teaspoon vanilla extract

Heat oven to 350°. Grease and flour two 9-inch round baking pans or 13×9×2-inch baking pan. In large mixer bowl combine flour, sugar, cocoa, baking soda, baking powder and salt. Add eggs, coffee, buttermilk, oil and vanilla; beat 2 minutes on medium speed (batter will be thin). Pour batter into prepared pan(s). Bake 30 to 35 minutes for round pans, 35 to 40 minutes for rectangular pan or until wooden pick inserted in center comes out clean. Cool 10 minutes; remove from pan(s) to wire rack. Cool completely; frost as desired.

10 to 12 servings

*To sour milk: Use 1 tablespoon white vinegar plus milk to equal 1 cup.

Chocolate Strawberry Shortcake

- 6 cups fresh strawberries
- 3/4 cup granulated sugar, divided
- 1 2/3 cups all-purpose flour
- 1/3 cup HERSHEY'S Cocoa
- 1 tablespoon baking powder
- 1/4 teaspoon salt
- 1/2 cup butter or margarine
- 1 egg, beaten
- 2/3 cup milk
- 1 cup chilled whipping cream
- 2 tablespoons confectioners' sugar

Select 6 strawberries; set aside. Slice remaining berries. Combine sliced berries and 1/4 cup granulated sugar; set aside. Heat oven to 450°. Grease 8-inch round baking pan. In medium bowl combine flour, cocoa, remaining 1/2 cup granulated sugar, baking powder and salt. Cut in butter until mixture resembles coarse crumbs. Combine egg and milk; add all at once to dry ingredients, stirring just to moisten. Spread dough in prepared pan, building up edges slightly. Bake 15 to 18 minutes. Cool 10 minutes. Remove from pan; place on serving plate. Beat whipping cream and confectioners' sugar until stiff. Arrange some sliced berries on top of cake. Spoon whipped cream over top. Garnish with reserved whole strawberries. Serve shortcake warm with remaining sliced strawberries. Garnish as desired. *8 servings*

All-Chocolate Boston Cream Pie

- 1 cup all-purpose flour
- 1 cup sugar
- 1/3 cup HERSHEY'S Cocoa
- 1/2 teaspoon baking soda
- 6 tablespoons butter or margarine, softened
- 1 cup milk
- 1 egg
- 1 teaspoon vanilla extract
- Chocolate Filling (recipe follows)
- Satiny Chocolate Glaze (recipe page 159)

Heat oven to 350°. Grease and flour 9-inch round baking pan. In large mixer bowl combine flour, sugar, cocoa and baking soda. Add butter, milk, egg and vanilla. Blend on low speed until all ingredients are moistened. Beat on medium speed 2 minutes or until mixture is smooth. Pour into prepared pan. Bake 30 to 35 minutes or until wooden pick inserted in center comes out clean. Cool 10 minutes; remove from pan. Cool completely. Meanwhile, prepare Chocolate Filling. Cut cake horizontally into two thin layers. Spread filling over one cake layer; top with remaining layer. Cover; chill. Pour Satiny Chocolate Glaze on top of cake, allowing some to drizzle down side. Cover; chill several hours. Garnish as desired. *8 servings*

Chocolate Filling

- 1/2 cup sugar
- 1/4 cup HERSHEY'S Cocoa
- 2 tablespoons cornstarch
- 1 1/2 cups light cream or half-and-half
- 1 tablespoon butter or margarine
- 1 teaspoon vanilla extract

In medium saucepan combine sugar, cocoa and cornstarch; gradually add light cream. Cook and stir over medium heat until mixture thickens and begins to boil; boil and stir 1 minute. Remove from heat; blend in butter and vanilla. Press plastic wrap directly onto surface. Cool completely.

Marble Cheesecake

- Chocolate Crumb Crust (recipe follows)
- 3 packages (8 ounces each) cream cheese, softened
- 1 cup sugar, divided
- 1/2 cup dairy sour cream
- 2 1/2 teaspoons vanilla extract, divided
- 3 tablespoons all-purpose flour
- 3 eggs
- 1/4 cup HERSHEY'S Cocoa
- 1 tablespoon vegetable oil

Prepare Chocolate Crumb Crust; set aside. Heat oven to 450°. In large mixer bowl combine cream cheese, 3/4 cup sugar, sour cream and 2 teaspoons vanilla; beat on medium speed until smooth. Gradually add flour; blend well. Add eggs and beat well; set aside. In small bowl combine cocoa and remaining

¼ cup sugar. Add oil, remaining ½ teaspoon vanilla and 1½ cups of cream cheese mixture; blend well. Spoon plain and chocolate mixtures alternately into cooled crust, ending with dollops of chocolate on top. Swirl gently with metal spatula or knife to marble. Bake 10 minutes. Without opening oven door, decrease temperature to 250° and continue to bake 30 minutes. Turn off oven; leave cheesecake in oven 30 minutes without opening door. Remove from oven; loosen cake from side of pan. Cool completely. Cover; chill. *10 to 12 servings*

Chocolate Crumb Crust

1 cup vanilla wafer crumbs (about 30 wafers)
¼ cup confectioners' sugar
¼ cup HERSHEY'S Cocoa
¼ cup butter or margarine, melted

Heat oven to 350°. In medium bowl stir together crumbs, confectioners' sugar and cocoa. Stir in butter. Press mixture onto bottom and ½ inch up side of 9-inch springform pan. Bake 8 minutes; cool.

Chocolatetown Special Cake

- 1/2 cup HERSHEY'S Cocoa
- 1/2 cup boiling water
- 2/3 cup shortening
- 1 3/4 cups sugar
- 1 teaspoon vanilla extract
- 2 eggs
- 2 1/4 cups all-purpose flour
- 1 1/2 teaspoons baking soda
- 1/2 teaspoon salt
- 1 1/3 cups buttermilk or sour milk*
- One-Bowl Buttercream Frosting (recipe follows)

In small bowl stir together cocoa and boiling water until smooth; set aside. Heat oven to 350°. Grease and flour two 9-inch round baking pans. In large mixer bowl cream shortening, sugar and vanilla until light and fluffy. Add eggs; beat well. Combine flour, baking soda and salt; add alternately with buttermilk to creamed mixture. Blend in cocoa mixture. Pour into prepared pans. Bake 35 to 40 minutes or until wooden pick inserted in center comes out clean. Cool 10 minutes; remove from pans. Cool completely; frost with One-Bowl Buttercream Frosting. Garnish as desired.

10 to 12 servings

*To sour milk: Use 1 tablespoon plus 1 teaspoon white vinegar plus milk to equal 1 1/3 cups.

One-Bowl Buttercream Frosting

- 6 tablespoons butter or margarine, softened
- HERSHEY'S Cocoa:
  - 1/3 cup for light flavor
  - 1/2 cup for medium flavor
  - 3/4 cup for dark flavor
- 2 2/3 cups confectioners' sugar
- 1/3 cup milk
- 1 teaspoon vanilla extract

In small mixer bowl cream butter. Add cocoa and confectioners' sugar alternately with milk; beat to spreading consistency (additional milk may be needed). Blend in vanilla.

About 2 cups frosting

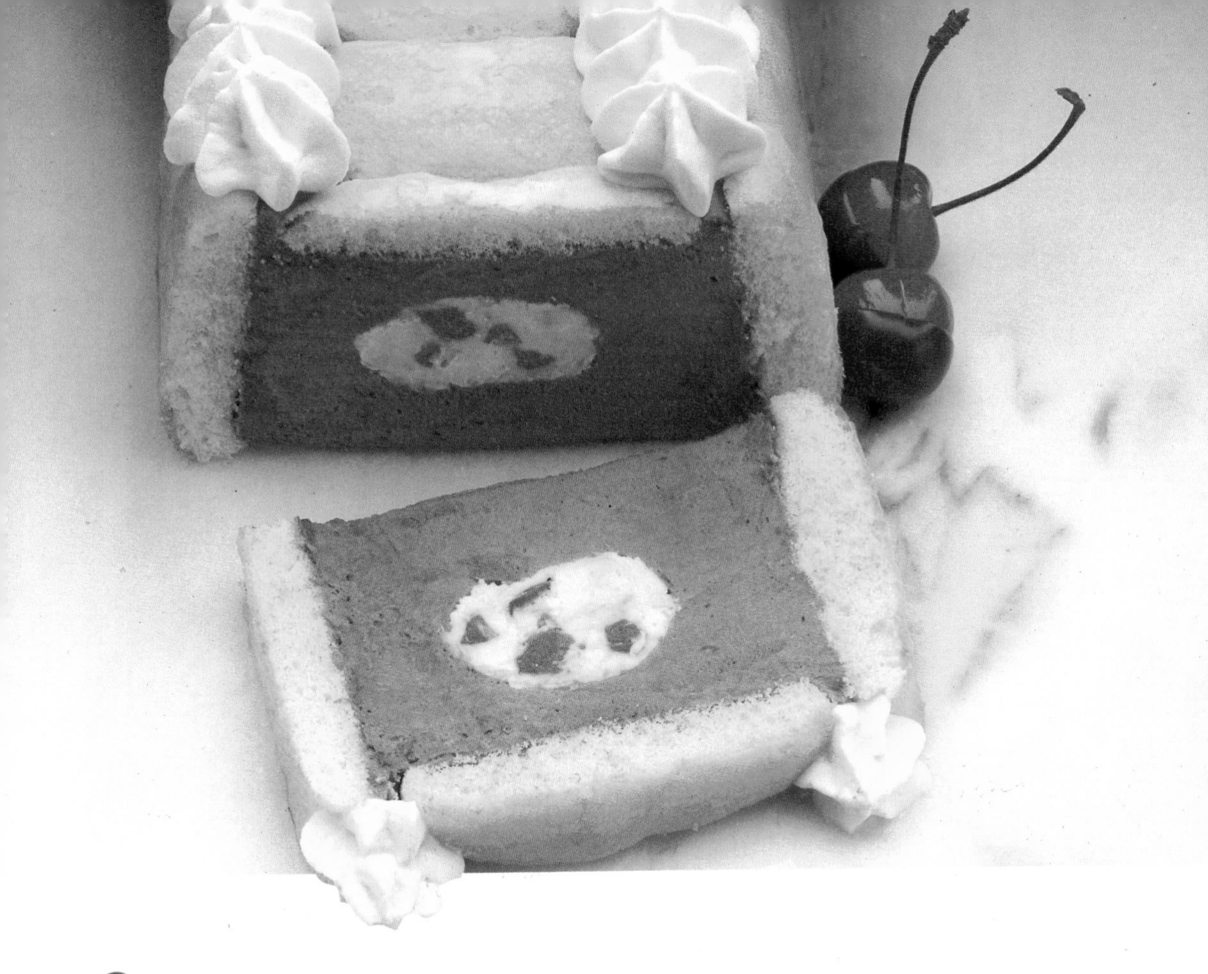

Chocolate Cherry Surprise

- 14 ladyfingers, split*
- 1 envelope unflavored gelatin
- 1/2 cup cold milk
- 1 package (8 ounces) cream cheese, softened
- 2/3 cup sugar
- 1 teaspoon vanilla extract
- 1/4 cup maraschino cherries, chopped
- 1/8 teaspoon almond extract
- 1/4 cup HERSHEY'S Cocoa
- 1 1/2 cups chilled whipping cream

Line 9 × 5 × 3-inch loaf pan with aluminum foil. Place ladyfingers on bottom and against sides of foil-lined pan, cutting to fit where necessary; set aside. In small saucepan sprinkle gelatin over milk; let stand 2 minutes to soften. Cook over low heat, stirring constantly, until gelatin is completely dissolved, about 5 minutes. In large mixer bowl beat cream cheese, sugar and vanilla until smooth. Blend in gelatin mixture; mix well. Remove 1/3 cup mixture to small bowl; stir in cherries and almond extract. Add cocoa to remaining mixture in large bowl, blending well. Beat whipping cream until stiff. Fold 1/2 cup whipped cream into cherry mixture; fold remaining whipped cream into chocolate. Spoon half of chocolate mixture into prepared pan. Using large serving spoon, make deep depression the length of chocolate mixture in pan. Spoon cherry mixture into depression, mounding slightly. Spoon in remaining chocolate mixture. Cover; chill about 4 hours or until set. To serve, unmold onto serving plate. Garnish as desired.

8 to 10 servings

*One 10 3/4-ounce frozen pound cake, thawed, and cut into 3/8-inch slices, may be substituted.

COOL DESSERTS

Soothing, refreshing desserts for everyday or for entertaining guests.

From left to right: Easy Double Chocolate Ice Cream, Creamy Smooth Choco-Blueberry Parfaits and Chocolate Mint Dessert (recipes page 62).

Chocolate Mint Dessert

1 cup all-purpose flour
1 cup sugar
1/2 cup butter or margarine, softened
4 eggs
1 1/2 cups (16-ounce can) HERSHEY'S Syrup
Mint Cream Center (recipe follows)
Chocolate Topping (recipe follows)

Heat oven to 350°. Grease 13 x 9 x 2-inch baking pan. In large mixer bowl combine flour, sugar, butter, eggs and syrup; beat until smooth. Pour into prepared pan; bake 25 to 30 minutes or until top springs back when touched lightly. Cool completely in pan. Spread Mint Cream Center on cake; cover and chill. Pour Chocolate Topping over chilled dessert. Cover; chill at least 1 hour before serving.

About 12 servings

Mint Cream Center

2 cups confectioners' sugar
1/2 cup butter or margarine, softened
2 tablespoons green creme de menthe*

In small mixer bowl combine confectioners' sugar, butter and creme de menthe; beat until smooth.

*1 tablespoon water, 1/2 to 3/4 teaspoon mint extract and 3 drops green food color may be substituted for creme de menthe.

Chocolate Topping

6 tablespoons butter or margarine
1 cup HERSHEY'S Semi-Sweet Chocolate Chips

In small saucepan over very low heat melt butter and chocolate chips. Remove from heat; stir until smooth. Cool slightly.

Creamy Smooth Choco-Blueberry Parfaits

1 package (6 ounces) instant chocolate pudding and pie filling
2 cups milk
1/2 cup HERSHEY'S Syrup
3 1/2 cups (8-ounce container) frozen non-dairy whipped topping, thawed
1 3/4 cups canned blueberry pie filling, chilled

In large mixer bowl combine pudding mix, milk and syrup; mix well. In separate bowl fold whipped topping into blueberry pie filling; reserve about 1 cup for garnish. Beginning with chocolate mixture, alternately layer with blueberry topping in parfait glasses. Cover and chill. Top with reserved blueberry topping. Garnish as desired.

6 to 8 parfaits

Easy Double Chocolate Ice Cream

2 cups chilled whipping cream
2 tablespoons HERSHEY'S Cocoa
1 can (14 ounces) sweetened condensed milk
1/3 cup HERSHEY'S Syrup

Line 9 x 5 x 3-inch loaf pan with foil. In large mixer bowl beat whipping cream and cocoa until stiff. Combine sweetened condensed milk and syrup; fold into whipped cream mixture. Pour into prepared pan. Cover; freeze 6 hours or until firm.

About 6 servings

Chocolate Frozen Dessert

- 1 package (16 ounces) chocolate sandwich cookies, crushed (about 1 3/4 cups)
- 1/2 cup butter or margarine, melted
- 1/2 gallon vanilla ice cream (in rectangular block)
- Chocolate Sauce (recipe follows)
- 2/3 cup pecan pieces (optional)

In medium bowl combine crushed cookies and butter. Press mixture onto bottom of 13 × 9 × 2-inch pan or two 8-inch square pans. Cut ice cream into 1/2-inch slices; place over crust. Cover; freeze 1 to 2 hours or until firm. Uncover pan(s); pour Chocolate Sauce over ice cream. Sprinkle pecan pieces over top, if desired. Cover; freeze until firm.

About 16 to 18 servings

Chocolate Sauce

- 2 cups confectioners' sugar
- 1/2 cup butter or margarine
- 1 1/2 cups (12-ounce can) evaporated milk
- 1 cup HERSHEY'S Semi-Sweet Chocolate Chips

In medium saucepan combine confectioners' sugar, butter, evaporated milk and chocolate chips. Cook over medium heat, stirring constantly, until mixture boils; boil and stir 8 minutes. Remove from heat; cool slightly.

About 2 1/2 cups

No-Bake Chocolate Cake Roll

- 1 package (3½ ounces) instant vanilla pudding and pie filling
- 3 tablespoons HERSHEY'S Cocoa, divided
- 1 cup milk
- 3½ cups (8-ounce container) frozen non-dairy whipped topping, thawed and divided
- 1 package (8½ ounces) crisp chocolate wafers (about 36)

In small mixer bowl combine pudding mix and 2 tablespoons cocoa. Add milk; beat on low speed until smooth and thickened. Fold in 1 cup whipped topping; blend well. Spread about 1 tablespoon pudding mixture onto each chocolate wafer. On foil, stack wafers on edges to form one long roll. Wrap tightly; chill at least 5 hours or overnight. Sift remaining 1 tablespoon cocoa over remaining 2½ cups whipped topping; blend well. Cover; refrigerate until just before serving. Unwrap roll; place on serving tray. Spread reserved whipped topping mixture over entire roll. To serve, cut diagonally in slices. Store, covered, in refrigerator. Garnish as desired.

About 8 servings

Chocolate-Marshmallow Mousse

- 1 bar (8 ounces) HERSHEY'S Milk Chocolate Bar
- 1½ cups miniature marshmallows
- ⅓ cup milk
- 1 cup chilled whipping cream

No-Bake Chocolate Cake Roll

Microwave Directions: Break chocolate bar into pieces; place in medium microwave-safe bowl with marshmallows and milk. Microwave at HIGH (100%) 1 to 1½ minutes or just until mixture is smooth when stirred; cool to room temperature. In small mixer bowl beat whipping cream until stiff; fold into cooled chocolate mixture. Pour into dessert dishes. Cover; chill 1 to 2 hours or until set. *6 servings*

VARIATIONS

Chocolate-Marshmallow Mousse Parfaits: Prepare Chocolate-Marshmallow Mousse according to directions. Alternately spoon mousse and sweetened whipped cream or whipped topping into parfait glasses. Cover; chill about 1 hour.

4 to 6 servings

Chocolate-Marshmallow Mousse Pie: Prepare Microwave Chocolate Crumb Crust (recipe follows) or use 8-inch (6 ounces) packaged chocolate flavored crumb crust. Prepare Chocolate-Marshmallow Mousse according to directions. Pour into crust. Cover; chill 2 to 3 hours or until firm. Garnish as desired.

8 servings

Microwave Chocolate Crumb Crust

Grease microwave-safe 9-inch pie plate. In small microwave-safe bowl place ½ cup butter or margarine. Microwave at HIGH (100%) about 1 minute or until melted. Stir in 1½ cups graham cracker crumbs, 6 tablespoons HERSHEY'S Cocoa and ⅓ cup confectioners' sugar until well blended. Press onto bottom and up sides of prepared pie plate. Microwave at HIGH 1 to 1½ minutes or until blistered; *do not overcook.* Cool completely before filling.

Easy Chocolate Sprinkled Ice Cream

- 3 egg yolks
- 1 can (14 ounces) sweetened condensed milk
- 3 tablespoons water
- 1 tablespoon vanilla extract
- 1 cup HERSHEY'S MINI CHIPS Semi-Sweet Chocolate
- 2 cups chilled whipping cream

Line 9 × 5 × 3-inch loaf pan with foil. In large bowl beat egg yolks with wire whisk; stir in sweetened condensed milk, water and vanilla. Finely chop MINI CHIPS Chocolate by hand or in food processor; set aside. In large mixer bowl beat whipping cream until stiff; fold with chopped chocolate into egg yolk mixture. Pour into prepared pan. Cover; freeze 6 hours or until firm.

About 6 servings

Easy Chocolate Sprinkled Ice Cream

Skor Toffee Candy Bar Ice Cream

- 3 egg yolks
- 1 can (14 ounces) sweetened condensed milk
- 3 tablespoons water
- 1 tablespoon vanilla extract
- 5 bars (1.4 ounces each) SKOR Toffee Candy Bar
- 2 cups chilled whipping cream

Line 9 × 5 × 3-inch loaf pan with foil. In large bowl beat egg yolks with wire whisk; stir in sweetened condensed milk, water and vanilla. Finely chop SKOR bars by hand or in food processor to measure 1¼ cups; set aside. In large mixer bowl beat whipping cream until stiff; fold with chopped SKOR Bars into egg yolk mixture. Pour into prepared pan. Cover; freeze 6 hours or until firm.

6 servings

Skor Toffee Candy Bar Ice Cream

Chocolate Rum Ice Cream

Chocolate Rum Ice Cream

- 1 cup sugar
- 2 tablespoons all-purpose flour
- 1 cup milk
- 1 egg, slightly beaten
- 2 squares (2 ounces) HERSHEY'S Unsweetened Baking Chocolate, broken into pieces
- ½ teaspoon rum extract
- 2 cups chilled light cream

Microwave Directions: In large microwave-safe bowl combine sugar and flour; gradually stir in milk. Blend in egg and baking chocolate pieces. Microwave at HIGH (100%) 2 to 2½ minutes, stirring frequently, just until mixture boils and thickens. Add rum extract; blend with wire whisk until mixture is smooth. Chill thoroughly. Add light cream to chilled mixture; blend well. Freeze in 2-quart ice cream freezer according to manufacturer's directions.

About 8 servings

Chocolate Mousse

1 teaspoon unflavored gelatin
1 tablespoon cold water
2 tablespoons boiling water
1/2 cup sugar
1/4 cup HERSHEY'S Cocoa
1 cup chilled whipping cream
1 teaspoon vanilla extract

In custard cup sprinkle gelatin over cold water; let stand 1 minute to soften. Add boiling water; stir until gelatin is completely dissolved and mixture is clear. Cool slightly. In small mixer bowl stir together sugar and cocoa; add whipping cream and vanilla. Beat at medium speed, scraping bottom of bowl occasionally, until stiff peaks form; pour in gelatin mixture and beat until well blended. Spoon into serving dishes. Chill about 1/2 hour.

Four 1/2 cup servings

Double Recipe: Use 1 envelope gelatin; double remaining ingredients. Follow directions above; use large mixer bowl.

VARIATIONS

Chocolate Mousse Pie: Prepare Double Recipe. Spoon mixture into 8-inch (6-ounces) packaged chocolate flavored crumb crust. Cover; chill at least 2 hours. Garnish with whipped cream, if desired. *6 to 8 servings*

Chocolate Mint Mousse in Chocolate Party Cups: Prepare one-half recipe Chocolate Party Cups (recipe page 194). Prepare Chocolate Mousse according to directions reducing vanilla extract to 1/2 teaspoon; add 1/8 to 1/4 teaspoon mint extract. Spoon or pipe mousse into chocolate cups; chill 2 to 3 hours. *6 servings*

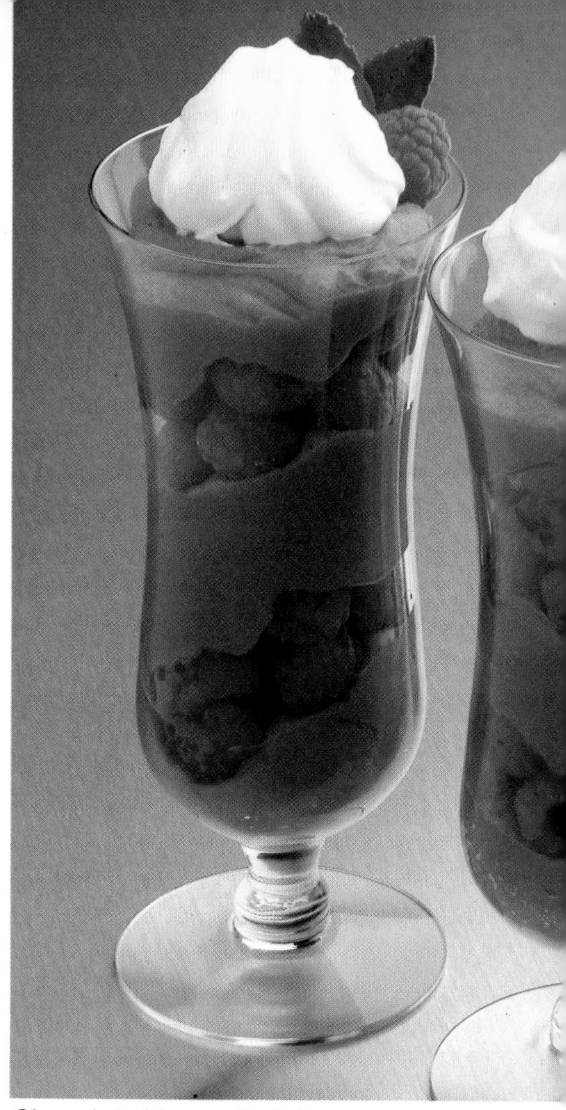

Chocolate Mousse Parfaits

Chocolate Mousse Parfaits: Prepare Chocolate Mousse according to directions. Alternately spoon mousse and sliced or diced fresh fruit into parfait glasses. (Strawberries, peaches or nectarines are good. About 1 1/2 cups prepared fruit will be needed.) Chill about 1 hour. *5 to 6 servings*

Variation: Substitute chilled cherry pie filling for fresh fruit.

Chocolate Mint Mousse in Chocolate Party Cups and Chocolate Mousse Filled Croissants

Chocolate Mousse Filled Croissants: Prepare Chocolate Mousse according to directions. Cut 6 bakery croissants horizontally in half. Spread about 1/3 cup mousse on each bottom half; replace top halves of croissants. Chill about 1/2 hour. To serve, top filled croissants with desired flavor canned fruit pie filling. *6 servings*

Pound Cake Torte: Prepare Chocolate Mousse according to directions. Slice loaf pound cake horizontally into 3 layers. Spread mousse evenly over one side of each cake layer. Stack layers. Chill 1 to 2 hours. Garnish with sliced nuts or fruit. *8 to 10 servings*

High-Rise Chocolate Mousse: Measure length of aluminum foil to fit around individual 3- or 4-ounce dessert dishes, custard cups or parfait glasses. Cut and fold foil to double thickness for collar. Lightly oil one side of foil; tape securely to outside of dish (oiled side in) allowing collar to extend 2 inches above rim. Prepare Double Recipe. Spoon mixture into prepared dishes. Chill 2 to 3 hours. Just before serving, carefully remove foil. Gently press chopped nuts onto side of mousse. *4 to 6 servings*

Chocolate Fried Ice Cream

- 1 quart vanilla ice cream
- 1 cup vanilla wafer crumbs
- 1/2 cup finely chopped pecans
- 1/2 cup flaked coconut
- 3 tablespoons HERSHEY'S Cocoa
- 2 eggs
- Vegetable oil
- Chocolate Nut Sauce (recipe follows)

With scoop form 6 ice cream balls. Place on wax paper-covered tray; cover and freeze several hours or until very firm. In medium bowl combine vanilla wafer crumbs, pecans, coconut and cocoa; set aside. In small bowl beat eggs. Coat ice cream balls with crumb mixture, pressing crumbs firmly into ice cream. Dip balls in beaten egg; coat again with crumb mixture. Place on wax paper-covered tray; freeze 2 hours or until very firm. Just before serving, heat 2 inches oil in heavy saucepan or deep fryer to 375°. Remove 2 balls at a time from freezer; fry in hot oil 20 to 25 seconds or until browned. Drain; serve immediately with Chocolate Nut Sauce. *6 servings*

Chocolate Nut Sauce

- 3 tablespoons butter or margarine
- 1/3 cup pecan pieces
- 2/3 cup sugar
- 1/4 cup HERSHEY'S Cocoa
- 1/8 teaspoon salt
- 1/2 cup light cream
- 1/2 teaspoon vanilla extract

In small saucepan over low heat melt butter. Saute pecans in melted butter until lightly browned. Remove from heat; stir in sugar, cocoa and salt. Add light cream; blend well. Cook over low heat, stirring constantly, until mixture just begins to boil. Remove from heat; add vanilla. Serve warm. *About 1 cup sauce*

Fudgey Decadence Pudding

- 2 squares (2 ounces) HERSHEY'S Unsweetened Baking Chocolate, finely chopped
- 1 cup light cream
- 2/3 cup sugar
- 2 egg yolks, slightly beaten
- 2 tablespoons butter or margarine
- 1 teaspoon vanilla extract

Microwave Directions: In medium microwave-safe bowl combine baking chocolate pieces and light cream. Microwave at HIGH (100%) 1 1/2 to 2 minutes or just until mixture is smooth when stirred. Microwave at HIGH about 1 minute or until mixture just begins to boil; stir in sugar. Microwave at HIGH about 1 minute or just until mixture begins to boil. With wire whisk gradually stir in beaten egg yolks; stir in butter and vanilla, blending well. Pour into creme pots or demitasse cups; press plastic wrap directly onto surface. Chill several hours or until set. Garnish as desired.

6 servings

Chocolate Butter Pecan Ice Cream

- 1/2 cup coarsely chopped pecans
- 1 tablespoon butter
- 1/2 cup HERSHEY'S Cocoa
- 2/3 cup water
- 1 can (14 ounces) sweetened condensed milk
- 2 teaspoons vanilla extract
- 2 cups chilled whipping cream

In small skillet over medium heat saute pecans in butter 2 minutes; set aside to cool. In small saucepan combine cocoa and water. Cook over medium heat, stirring constantly, until mixture boils. Remove from heat; stir in sweetened condensed milk and vanilla. Pour into 9-inch square pan; freeze until slushy. In large mixer bowl beat cream until stiff. In small chilled bowl whip chocolate mixture; fold into whipped cream. Stir in pecans. Return to square pan; cover and return to freezer. Freeze until firm, 2 to 3 hours, stirring frequently during first hour.

About 1 1/2 quarts ice cream

Chocolate Butter Pecan Ice Cream

Peanut Butter Sundae Pie

- No-Bake Chocolate Crumb Crust (recipe follows)
- 1 quart vanilla ice cream
- Peanut Butter Chip Ice Cream Sauce (recipe follows)

Prepare No-Bake Chocolate Crumb Crust. Cover; freeze. Place scoops of ice cream into crust. Cover; freeze until just before serving. Serve with Peanut Butter Chip Ice Cream Sauce.

8 servings

No-Bake Chocolate Crumb Crust

In small bowl combine 1 1/4 cups graham cracker crumbs, 1/4 cup HERSHEY'S Cocoa, 1/4 cup sugar and 1/3 cup melted butter or margarine. Press mixture onto bottom and up sides of buttered 9-inch pie plate.

Peanut Butter Chip Ice Cream Sauce

- 1 cup REESE'S Peanut Butter Chips
- 1/3 cup evaporated milk
- 2 tablespoons light corn syrup
- 1 tablespoon butter or margarine
- 1 teaspoon vanilla extract

Microwave Directions: In small microwave-safe bowl combine peanut butter chips, evaporated milk, corn syrup and butter; stir. Microwave at HIGH (100%) 1 to 1 1/2 minutes or until chips are softened; stir with whisk until chips are melted and mixture is smooth. Stir in vanilla. Cool slightly.

About 3/4 cup sauce

Conventional Directions: In small saucepan combine all ingredients except vanilla. Cook over low heat, stirring constantly, until chips are melted and mixture is smooth. Stir in vanilla. Cool slightly.

Chocolate Coeur a la Creme with Strawberry Sauce

- 1/2 cup whipping cream, divided
- 3 tablespoons HERSHEY'S Cocoa
- 1 tablespoon butter
- 1 package (3 ounces) cream cheese, softened
- 1/2 cup confectioner's sugar
- 1/2 teaspoon vanilla extract
- Strawberry Sauce (recipe follows)

Line two 1/2-cup coeur a la creme molds or two 6-ounce custard cups with double thickness of dampened cheese cloth, extending far enough beyond edges to enclose filling completely. In small saucepan combine 1/4 cup whipping cream, cocoa and butter; cook over low heat, stirring constantly, until smooth. Remove from heat; cool. In small mixer bowl beat cream cheese, confectioners' sugar and vanilla until smooth. Add cocoa mixture, blending well. Beat in remaining 1/4 cup whipping cream. Spoon mixture into prepared molds. Fold cheesecloth over top. Place molds on wire rack set in tray or deep plate. Refrigerate 8 hours or overnight. To serve, pull back cheesecloth and invert each mold onto a chilled dessert plate; carefully remove cheesecloth. Serve with Strawberry Sauce.

8 servings

Strawberry Sauce

- 1 package (10 ounces) frozen strawberries in lite syrup, thawed
- 1 tablespoon kirsch (optional)

In food processor or blender container puree strawberries. Strain through fine sieve into small bowl. Stir in kirsch, if desired.

About 1 cup sauce

Chocolate Pots de Creme

2/3 cup sugar
6 tablespoons HERSHEY'S Cocoa
1 cup light cream
2 egg yolks, slightly beaten
1/4 cup butter, softened
1 teaspoon vanilla extract
Sweetened whipped cream

In medium saucepan combine sugar and cocoa; gradually add light cream. Cook over medium heat, stirring constantly, just until mixture comes to a boil. Remove from heat; gradually stir into beaten egg yolks. Stir in butter and vanilla; blend well. Pour into 6 creme pots or demitasse cups; press plastic wrap directly onto surface. Chill several hours or until set. Garnish with sweetened whipped cream.

6 servings

Chocolate Frozen Yogurt

1/4 cup HERSHEY'S Cocoa
1/4 cup sugar
2 containers (8 ounces each) vanilla yogurt
1/4 cup light corn syrup

In medium bowl combine cocoa and sugar. Add yogurt and corn syrup; stir until well blended and smooth. Pour mixture into 8-inch square pan or 9×5×3-inch loaf pan. Cover; freeze several hours or overnight until firm. Spoon into large mixer bowl. With mixer on low speed, beat until smooth but not melted. Return to pan or pour into 1 pint freezer container. Cover; freeze several hours or overnight until firm. Before serving, allow to stand at room temperature about 10 minutes.

About 4 servings

Chocolate Pots de Creme

Choco-Berry Frozen Dessert (left) and Cherry Crowned Cocoa Pudding

Choco-Berry Frozen Dessert

- 3 packages (3 ounces each) cream cheese, softened and divided
- 1 cup HERSHEY'S Syrup
- 1/2 cup water
- 4 1/2 cups (about 12 ounces) frozen non-dairy whipped topping, thawed and divided
- 3/4 cup pureed strawberries (fresh, sweetened OR frozen, thawed and drained berries)

Line 9 × 5 × 3-inch loaf pan with foil. In large mixer bowl beat 2 packages cream cheese. Blend in syrup and water; beat until smooth. Fold in 3 cups whipped topping. Spoon half of chocolate mixture into prepared pan; freeze 15 minutes. Chill remaining chocolate mixture. In small mixer bowl beat remaining package cream cheese. Blend in strawberries until smooth. Fold in remaining 1 1/2 cups whipped topping. Spoon strawberry mixture over chocolate layer in pan. Top with chilled chocolate mixture. Cover; freeze several hours or overnight until firm. Unmold about 10 minutes before serving. Peel off foil before slicing.

About 10 servings

Fruited Chocolate Sorbet

1 ripe, medium banana
1 1/2 cups orange juice
1/2 cup sugar
1/4 cup HERSHEY'S Cocoa
1 cup chilled whipping cream

Slice banana into blender container. Add orange juice; blend until smooth. Add sugar and cocoa; blend until thoroughly combined. Add whipping cream; blend well. Pour mixture into 9-inch square pan. Freeze until hard around edges. Spoon mixture into large mixer bowl or blender container; blend until smooth. Pour into 1-quart mold. Freeze 4 to 6 hours or until firm. To serve, unmold onto chilled plate; cut into slices. *About 8 servings*

Cherry-Crowned Cocoa Pudding

1 cup sugar
1/2 cup HERSHEY'S Cocoa
1/3 cup all-purpose biscuit baking mix
2 cups milk
1 cup water
1 can (21 ounces) cherry pie filling, chilled

In medium saucepan combine sugar, cocoa and baking mix. Stir in milk and water. Cook over medium heat, stirring constantly, until mixture comes to full boil; remove from heat. Pour into dessert dishes. Press plastic wrap directly onto surface. Chill several hours or until set. Garnish with cherry pie filling. *6 servings*

Fast Fudge Pots de Creme

1 package (3 1/2 ounces) chocolate pudding and pie filling
2 cups milk
1 cup HERSHEY'S Semi-Sweet Chocolate Chips or MINI CHIPS

In medium saucepan combine pudding mix and milk. Cook over medium heat, stirring constantly, until mixture comes to full boil; remove from heat. Stir in chocolate chips until melted and mixture is smooth. Spoon into 8 creme pots or demitasse cups. Press plastic wrap directly onto surface. Serve slightly warm or chilled. Garnish as desired. *8 servings*

Chocolate-Covered Banana Pops

3 ripe, large bananas
9 wooden ice cream sticks or skewers
2 cups (12-ounce package) HERSHEY'S Semi-Sweet Chocolate Chips
2 tablespoons shortening
1 1/2 cups coarsely chopped unsalted, roasted peanuts

Peel bananas; cut each into thirds. Insert wooden stick into each banana piece; place on wax paper-covered tray. Cover; freeze until firm. In top of double boiler over hot, not boiling, water melt chocolate chips and shortening. Remove bananas from freezer just before dipping. Dip each piece into warm chocolate, covering completely; allow excess to drip off. Immediately roll in peanuts. Cover; return to freezer. Serve frozen.

9 pops

Chocolate Cream Squares

Chocolate Graham Crust (recipe follows)
1 package (3 ounces) cream cheese, softened
2/3 cup sugar
1 teaspoon vanilla extract
1/3 cup HERSHEY'S Cocoa
1/3 cup milk
1 container (8-ounces) frozen non-dairy whipped topping, thawed

Prepare Chocolate Graham Crust; reserve 1/4 cup crumbs. Press remaining crumbs onto bottom of 9-inch square pan; set aside. In small mixer bowl beat cream cheese, sugar and vanilla until well blended. Add cocoa alternately with milk, beating until smooth. Gradually fold in whipped topping until well combined. Spoon mixture over crust. Sprinkle reserved crumbs over top. Cover; chill 6 to 8 hours or until set. Cut into squares. *6 to 9 servings*

Chocolate Graham Crust

In medium bowl, stir together 1 1/4 cups graham cracker crumbs, 1/4 cup HERSHEY'S Cocoa, 1/4 cup sugar and 1/3 cup melted butter or margarine.

Three-In-One Chocolate Pudding & Pie Filling

- 3/4 cup sugar
- 1/3 cup HERSHEY'S Cocoa
- 2 tablespoons cornstarch
- 2 tablespoons all-purpose flour
- 1/4 teaspoon salt
- 2 cups milk
- 2 egg yolks, slightly beaten
- 2 tablespoons butter or margarine
- 1 teaspoon vanilla extract

In medium saucepan combine sugar, cocoa, cornstarch, flour and salt; blend in milk and egg yolks. Cook over medium heat, stirring constantly, until mixture boils; boil and stir 1 minute. Remove from heat; blend in butter and vanilla. Pour into medium bowl or individual serving dishes; press plastic wrap directly onto surface. Cool; chill.

4 servings

Pie: Reduce milk to 1 3/4 cups; cook as directed. Pour hot pudding into 8-inch (6 ounces) packaged graham crumb crust; press plastic wrap onto surface. Chill; top with sweetened whipped cream or whipped topping before serving. *6 servings*

Parfaits: Alternate layers of cold pudding and sweetened whipped cream in parfait glasses.

Microwave Directions: In 2-quart microwave-safe bowl combine sugar, cocoa, cornstarch, flour and salt; blend in milk and egg yolks. Microwave at HIGH (100%) 5 minutes, stirring several times, or until mixture boils. Microwave at HIGH 1 to 2 additional minutes or until mixture is smooth and thickened. Stir in butter and vanilla.

Chocolate-Amaretto Ice

Banana Fudge Pops

1 ripe, medium banana
1 1/2 cups orange-banana juice
1/2 cup sugar
1/4 cup HERSHEY'S Cocoa
1 can (5 ounces) evaporated milk
6 paper cold drink cups (5 ounces each)
6 wooden popsicle sticks

Slice banana into blender container; add juice. Cover; blend until smooth. Add sugar and cocoa; cover and blend well. Add evaporated milk; cover and blend. Pour mixture into cups. Freeze about 1 hour; insert popsicle sticks into fudge pops. Cover; freeze until firm. Peel off cups to serve. *6 pops*

Chocolate-Amaretto Ice

3/4 cup sugar
1/2 cup HERSHEY'S Cocoa
2 cups light cream or half-and-half
2 tablespoons almond-flavored liqueur
Sliced almonds

In small saucepan combine sugar and cocoa; gradually stir in light cream. Cook over low heat, stirring constantly, until sugar dissolves and mixture is smooth and hot; do not boil. Remove from heat; stir in liqueur. Pour into 8-inch square pan. Cover; freeze until firm, stirring several times before mixture freezes. Scoop into dessert dishes. Serve frozen with sliced almonds. Garnish as desired. *4 servings*

Banana Fudge Pops

"The Best" Chocolate Ice Cream

- 2 eggs
- 2 cups sugar, divided
- 2/3 cup HERSHEY'S Cocoa
- 2 tablespoons cornstarch
- 1/4 teaspoon salt
- 2 cups milk
- 1 tablespoon vanilla extract
- 4 cups light cream
- 1 cup whipping cream

In small mixer bowl combine eggs and 1/2 cup sugar; beat well. In large saucepan combine remaining 1 1/2 cups sugar, cocoa, cornstarch and salt; gradually stir in milk. Cook over medium heat, stirring constantly, until mixture boils; boil and stir 1 minute. Blend about half of hot mixture into beaten eggs. Stir hot mixture into saucepan. Blend in vanilla, light cream and whipping cream. Chill thoroughly. Fill ice cream freezer container 2/3 full; freeze according to manufacturer's directions. Remove lid; take out dasher. Pack mixture down; replace lid. Repack in ice and salt. Let stand several hours to ripen.

About 3 quarts ice cream

VARIATIONS

After ice cream is frozen, remove dasher; allow ice cream to ripen 1 hour. Prepare one of the following additions. Gradually add to partially ripened ice cream, swirling gently to marble. If a more firm ice cream is desired, allow additional time to ripen.

Chocolate-Marshmallow: Combine 2 cups marshmallow creme with 2 tablespoons milk. Add as directed above.

Chocolate-Peppermint: Crush hard peppermint candies to equal 3/4 cup. Add as directed above.

From top to bottom: "The Best" Chocolate Ice Cream, Chocolate-Marshmallow Ice Cream and Chocolate-Peppermint Ice Cream

Chocolate-Peanut Butter: In small saucepan combine 1 1/2 cups REESE'S Peanut Butter Chips, 1/2 cup sugar and 1/2 cup milk. Stir over low heat until well blended; cool. Add as directed above.

PIES

A tantalizing selection of pies—all easy to make, and easy to enjoy.

Chocolate Grasshopper Pie
(recipe page 82)

Chocolate Grasshopper Pie

Microwave Chocolate Crumb Crust (recipe follows) OR 8-inch (6 ounces) packaged chocolate flavored crumb crust
3 cups miniature marshmallows
1/2 cup milk
1/4 cup HERSHEY'S Cocoa
2 tablespoons white creme de menthe
2 tablespoons white creme de cacao
1 cup chilled whipping cream
2 tablespoons confectioners' sugar

Prepare crust, if desired; set aside. In medium saucepan combine marshmallows, milk and cocoa. Stir constantly over low heat until marshmallows are melted; remove from heat. Stir in creme de menthe and creme de cacao; cool to room temperature. In small mixer bowl beat whipping cream with confectioners' sugar until stiff. Fold in cooled chocolate mixture. Spoon into crust. Cover and freeze several hours or overnight. Garnish as desired. *6 to 8 servings*

Microwave Chocolate Crumb Crust

Grease microwave-safe 9-inch pie plate. In small microwave-safe bowl place 1/2 cup butter or margarine. Microwave at HIGH (100%) about 1 minute or until melted. Stir in 1 1/2 cups graham cracker crumbs, 6 tablespoons HERSHEY'S Cocoa and 1/3 cup confectioners' sugar until well blended. Press onto bottom and up sides of prepared pie plate. Microwave at HIGH 1 to 1 1/2 minutes or until blistered; *do not overcook.* Cool completely before filling.

Fudge Satin Pie

1 cup HERSHEY'S Semi-Sweet Chocolate Chips or MINI CHIPS
4 eggs, separated and at room temperature
1/4 teaspoon cream of tartar
1/4 cup sugar
1 teaspoon vanilla extract
8-inch (6 ounces) packaged crumb crust
Whipped topping
Chocolate curls

In top of double boiler over hot, not boiling, water melt chocolate chips, stirring constantly to blend. (OR in small microwave-safe bowl place chips. Microwave at HIGH (100%) 1 minute; stir. If necessary, microwave at HIGH additional 15 seconds or until melted and smooth when stirred.) In small mixer bowl slightly beat egg yolks. Gradually add melted chocolate, beating well after each addition; set aside. Using clean beaters and large mixer bowl, beat egg whites and cream of tartar until foamy. Gradually add sugar and vanilla, beating until stiff peaks form. Fold in chocolate mixture. Pour into crust. Cover; chill several hours or overnight. Garnish with whipped topping and chocolate curls.
6 to 8 servings

Chocolate Cheese Pie

Chocolate Cheese Pie

- 1 package (8 ounces) cream cheese, softened
- 1 package (3 ounces) cream cheese, softened
- 3/4 cup sugar
- 1 teaspoon vanilla extract
- 1/4 cup HERSHEY'S Cocoa
- 2 eggs
- 1/2 cup whipping cream
- 8-inch (6 ounces) packaged crumb crust
- Cherry pie or peach pie filling

Heat oven to 350°. In large mixer bowl beat cream cheese, sugar and vanilla until well blended. Blend in cocoa, scraping sides of bowl and beaters frequently. Add eggs; blend well. Blend in whipping cream. Pour into crust. Bake 35 to 40 minutes. (Center will be soft but will set upon cooling). Cool to room temperature. Cover; chill several hours or overnight. Serve with pie filling.

6 to 8 servings

Chocolate Pecan Pie

- 9-inch unbaked pastry shell
- 1 cup sugar
- 1/3 cup HERSHEY'S Cocoa
- 3 eggs, slightly beaten
- 1 cup light corn syrup
- 1 tablespoon butter or margarine, melted
- 1 teaspoon vanilla extract
- 1 cup pecan halves
- Whipped topping

Prepare pastry shell; set aside. Heat oven to 350°. In medium bowl combine sugar and cocoa. Add eggs, corn syrup, butter and vanilla; stir until well blended. Stir in pecans. Pour into unbaked pastry shell. Bake 60 minutes. Cool completely. Garnish with whipped topping. *8 servings*

Banana Split Pie

Crumb-Nut Crust (recipe follows)
1 1/4 cups sugar
1/3 cup cornstarch
1/3 cup HERSHEY'S Cocoa
1/4 teaspoon salt
2 1/2 cups milk
2 egg yolks, slightly beaten
3 tablespoons butter or margarine
1 teaspoon vanilla extract
2 medium ripe bananas, sliced
Frozen whipped topping, thawed
Chopped peanuts
Additional banana slices
Maraschino cherries

Prepare Crumb-Nut Crust. In medium saucepan stir together sugar, cornstarch, cocoa and salt. Blend milk and egg yolks; gradually stir into sugar mixture. Cook over medium heat, stirring constantly, until mixture thickens and boils. Boil and stir over low heat 3 minutes. Remove from heat, blend in butter and vanilla. Press plastic wrap directly onto filling; cool about 20 minutes. Arrange banana slices over bottom of crust. Pour filling over bananas; press plastic wrap onto filling. Refrigerate 3 to 4 hours. Remove plastic wrap; top pie with dollops of whipped topping. Garnish with chopped peanuts, banana slices and maraschino cherries. *8 servings*

Crumb-Nut Crust

1 1/4 cups graham cracker crumbs
1/3 cup butter or margarine, melted
1/4 cup finely chopped peanuts

Heat oven to 350°. In medium bowl combine all ingredients; press evenly onto bottom and up sides of 9-inch pie plate. Bake 8 to 10 minutes; cool.

Fudgey Pecan Pie

9-inch unbaked pastry shell
1/3 cup butter or margarine
1/3 cup HERSHEY'S Cocoa
2/3 cup sugar
1/4 teaspoon salt
3 eggs, slightly beaten
3/4 cup light corn syrup
1 cup chopped pecans (optional)
1 cup pecan halves
Sweetened Whipped Cream (recipe follows)

Prepare pastry shell; set aside. Heat oven to 375°. In medium saucepan over low heat melt butter; add cocoa and stir until mixture is smooth. Remove from heat; cool slightly. Stir in sugar, salt, eggs and corn syrup; blend thoroughly. Stir in chopped pecans, if desired. Pour into unbaked pastry shell. Place pecan halves over top. Bake 40 minutes. Cool. Cover; let stand about 8 hours before serving. Garnish with Sweetened Whipped Cream.

8 servings

Sweetened Whipped Cream

In small mixer bowl combine 1/2 cup chilled whipping cream, 1 tablespoon confectioners' sugar and 1/4 teaspoon vanilla extract; beat until stiff. *About 1 cup topping*

Cocoa Cloud Pie

2 packages (3 ounces each) cream cheese, softened
1 cup confectioners' sugar
2 teaspoons vanilla extract
1/2 cup HERSHEY'S Cocoa
1/4 cup milk
2 cups chilled whipping cream
8-inch (6 ounces) packaged crumb crust

In large mixer bowl beat cream cheese, confectioners' sugar and vanilla until well blended. Add cocoa alternately with milk, beating until smooth. Gradually add whipping cream, beating until stiff. Spoon into crust. Cover; chill several hours or overnight. Garnish as desired. *6 to 8 servings*

Peanut Butter Tarts

1 package (3 1/2 ounces) instant vanilla pudding and pie filling
1 1/2 cups milk, divided
1 cup REESE'S Peanut Butter Chips
6 (4-ounce package) single serve graham crusts
Whipped topping
Fresh fruit

In small mixer bowl blend pudding mix and 1 cup milk; set aside. In top of double boiler over hot, not boiling, water melt peanut butter chips with remaining 1/2 cup milk, stirring constantly to blend. (OR in small microwave-safe bowl place chips and 1/2 cup milk. Microwave at HIGH (100%) 45 seconds; stir. If necessary, microwave at HIGH additional 15 seconds or until melted and smooth when stirred.) Gradually add to pudding, blending well. Spoon into crusts. Cover; chill until set. Garnish with whipped topping and fruit.
6 servings

Individual Chocolate Cream Pies

1 1/2 ounces (1/2 of 3-ounce package) cream cheese, softened
6 tablespoons sugar
1/2 teaspoon vanilla extract
2 1/2 tablespoons HERSHEY'S Cocoa
2 1/2 tablespoons milk
1 cup chilled whipping cream
6 (4-ounce package) single serve graham crusts
Whipped topping
HERSHEY'S MINI CHIPS Semi-Sweet Chocolate

In small mixer bowl beat cream cheese, sugar and vanilla until well blended. Add cocoa alternately with milk, beating until smooth. In separate bowl beat whipping cream until stiff; fold into chocolate mixture. Spoon into crusts. Cover; chill until set. Garnish with whipped topping and MINI CHIPS Chocolate.
6 servings

From top to bottom: Cocoa Cloud Pie, Peanut Butter Tarts and Individual Chocolate Cream Pies

Bavarian Chocolate Pie

Bavarian Chocolate Pie

9-inch baked pastry shell or crumb crust
1 envelope unflavored gelatin
1 2/3 cups milk, divided
2/3 cup sugar
1/3 cup HERSHEY'S Cocoa
2 tablespoons butter or margarine
3/4 teaspoon vanilla extract
1/2 cup chilled whipping cream
Spiced Cream (recipe page 91)

Prepare pastry shell; cool. In medium saucepan sprinkle gelatin over 1 cup milk; let stand 2 minutes to soften. Combine sugar and cocoa; add to gelatin mixture in saucepan. Cook over low heat, stirring constantly, until mixture boils. Remove from heat; add butter and stir until melted. Blend in remaining 2/3 cup milk and vanilla. Cool; chill, stirring occasionally, until mixture begins to set. Beat cream until stiff; carefully fold into chocolate mixture. Pour into baked pastry shell; chill 2 to 3 hours or until set. Garnish with Spiced Cream. *8 servings*

Coffee Butter-Crunch Pie

Chocolate Nut Crust (recipe follows)
2 teaspoons powdered instant coffee
1 teaspoon boiling water
1/2 cup unsalted butter, softened
3/4 cup packed light brown sugar
3 tablespoons HERSHEY'S Cocoa
2 eggs
Topping (recipe follows)

Prepare Chocolate Nut Crust. Dissolve instant coffee in water; set aside. In small mixer bowl cream butter. Add sugar; beat on medium speed 3 minutes. Beat in cocoa and coffee mixture. Add eggs, one at a time, beating 5 minutes after each addition, scraping sides of bowl occasionally. Pour filling into cooled crust. Cover and chill 5 to 6 hours. Spoon dollops of Topping on top of filling, or spread Topping evenly over filling. Chill 1 hour or until serving time. Garnish as desired. Refrigerate leftovers. *8 servings*

Chocolate Nut Crust

1 1/3 cups pie crust mix (1/2 of 11-ounce package)
1/4 cup packed light brown sugar
3 tablespoons HERSHEY'S Cocoa
3/4 cup finely chopped walnuts
1 tablespoon water
1 tablespoon vegetable oil
1 teaspoon vanilla extract

Heat oven to 375°. In medium bowl combine pie crust mix, sugar and cocoa. Stir in walnuts. Combine water, oil and vanilla; drizzle over pie crust mixture while stirring with fork. (Mixture will be crumbly.) Press mixture evenly onto bottom and up sides of 9-inch pie plate. Bake 15 minutes; cool.

Topping

In small mixer bowl combine 1/2 cup chilled whipping cream, 1 tablespoon confectioners' sugar and 1/4 teaspoon vanilla extract; beat until stiff. *About 1 cup topping*

VARIATIONS

Mile High Topping: In large mixer bowl combine 2 cups chilled whipping cream, 1/4 cup confectioners' sugar and 1 teaspoon vanilla extract; beat just until cream holds a definite shape. Do not over beat. *About 4 cups topping*

Mile High Coffee-Flavored Topping: Increase confectioners' sugar to 1/2 cup. Add 1 to 2 tablespoons powdered instant coffee. Follow directions above.

Coffee Butter Crunch Pie

From left to right: Two-Tone Cream Pie, Chocolate Chip Walnut Pie and Double Chocolate Mocha Pie

Two-Tone Cream Pie

- 9-inch baked pastry shell
- 1 package (4 3/4 ounces) vanilla pudding and pie filling
- 3 1/2 cups milk
- 1 cup REESE'S Peanut Butter Chips
- 1 cup HERSHEY'S Semi-Sweet Chocolate Chips or MINI CHIPS

Prepare pastry shell; cool. In medium saucepan combine pudding mix and milk. Cook over medium heat, stirring constantly, until mixture comes to full boil; remove from heat. Pour 2 cups hot pudding into small bowl and add peanut butter chips; stir until chips are melted and mixture is smooth. To remaining hot pudding, add chocolate chips; stir until chips are melted and mixture is smooth. Pour chocolate mixture into baked pastry shell. Gently pour and spread peanut butter mixture over top. Press plastic wrap directly onto surface. Chill several hours or overnight. Garnish as desired.

8 servings

Chocolate Chip Walnut Pie

- 9-inch baked pastry shell
- 3/4 cup packed light brown sugar
- 1/2 cup all-purpose flour
- 1/2 teaspoon baking powder
- 1/4 teaspoon ground cinnamon
- 2 eggs, slightly beaten
- 1 cup HERSHEY'S Semi-Sweet Chocolate Chips, MINI CHIPS or Milk Chocolate Chips
- 1 cup coarsely chopped walnuts
- Spiced Cream (recipe follows)

Prepare pastry shell; cool. Heat oven to 350°. In medium bowl combine brown sugar, flour, baking powder and cinnamon. Add eggs; stir until well blended. Add chocolate chips and walnuts. Pour into baked pastry shell. Bake 25 to 30 minutes or until lightly browned and set. Serve slightly warm or at room temperature with Spiced Cream. *8 servings*

Spiced Cream

In small mixer bowl combine 1/2 cup chilled whipping cream, 1 tablespoon confectioners' sugar, 1/4 teaspoon vanilla extract, 1/4 teaspoon ground cinnamon and dash ground nutmeg; beat until stiff. *About 1 cup topping*

Double Chocolate Mocha Pie

- 1 package (6 ounces) instant chocolate pudding and pie filling
- 2 2/3 cups HERSHEY'S Chocolate Milk
- 8-inch (6 ounces) packaged crumb crust
- Coffee Whipped Cream (recipe follows)

In large mixer bowl beat pudding mix and chocolate milk until blended. Pour into crust. Cover and chill several hours or overnight. Serve with dollops of Coffee Whipped Cream. Garnish as desired.

6 to 8 servings

Coffee Whipped Cream

In small mixer bowl combine 1 cup chilled whipping cream, 1/4 cup confectioners' sugar, 1 tablespoon powdered instant coffee and 1/2 teaspoon vanilla extract. Beat just until cream holds definite shape; *do not overbeat.*

About 2 cups topping

Hershey's Syrup Pie

- 9-inch baked pastry shell
- 2 egg yolks
- 1/3 cup cornstarch
- 1/4 teaspoon salt
- 1 3/4 cups milk
- 1 cup HERSHEY'S Syrup
- 1 teaspoon vanilla extract
- Syrup Whipped Topping (recipe follows)
- Fresh fruit

Microwave Directions: Prepare pastry shell; cool. In medium microwave-safe bowl beat egg yolks. Add cornstarch, salt, milk and syrup; blend well. Microwave at MEDIUM-HIGH (70%) 6 to 8 minutes, stirring every 2 minutes with whisk, or until mixture is smooth and very thick. Stir in vanilla. Pour into baked pastry shell. Press plastic wrap directly onto surface; chill several hours or overnight. Garnish with Syrup Whipped Topping and fresh fruit.

6 to 8 servings

Syrup Whipped Topping

In small mixer bowl combine 1 cup chilled whipping cream, 1/2 cup HERSHEY'S Syrup, 2 tablespoons confectioners' sugar and 1/2 teaspoon vanilla extract. Beat just until cream holds definite shape; *do not overbeat.*

About 2 1/4 cups topping

Fudge Brownie Pie

- 2 eggs
- 1 cup sugar
- 1/2 cup butter or margarine, melted
- 1/2 cup all-purpose flour
- 1/3 cup HERSHEY'S Cocoa
- 1/4 teaspoon salt
- 1 teaspoon vanilla extract
- 1/2 cup chopped nuts (optional)
- Ice Cream
- Hot Fudge Sauce (recipe follows)

Heat oven to 350°. Lightly grease 8-inch pie plate. In small mixer bowl beat eggs; blend in sugar and butter. Combine flour, cocoa and salt; add to butter mixture. Stir in vanilla and nuts, if desired. Pour into prepared pie plate. Bake 25 to 30 minutes or until almost set. (Pie will not test done in center.) Cool; cut into wedges. Serve topped with scoop of ice cream and drizzled with Hot Fudge Sauce. *6 to 8 servings*

Hot Fudge Sauce

- 3/4 cup sugar
- 1/2 cup HERSHEY'S Cocoa
- 1/2 cup plus 2 tablespoons (5-ounce can) evaporated milk
- 1/3 cup light corn syrup
- 1/3 cup butter or margarine
- 1 teaspoon vanilla extract

In small saucepan combine sugar and cocoa; blend in evaporated milk and corn syrup. Cook over medium heat, stirring constantly, until mixture boils; boil and stir 1 minute. Remove from heat; stir in butter and vanilla. Serve warm.

About 1 3/4 cups sauce

Microwave Directions: In medium microwave-safe bowl combine all sauce ingredients except butter and vanilla. Microwave at HIGH (100%) 1 to 3 minutes, stirring often, until mixture boils. Stir in butter and vanilla. Cool slightly; serve warm.

Creme de Cacao Pie

- 9-inch baked pastry shell
- 1 envelope unflavored gelatin
- 1/2 cup cold milk
- 1/4 cup butter or margarine
- 2/3 cup sugar, divided
- 6 tablespoons HERSHEY'S Cocoa
- 3 eggs, separated
- 1/4 cup creme de cacao

Prepare pastry shell; cool. In small bowl sprinkle gelatin over milk; let stand 5 minutes to soften. In medium saucepan over low heat melt butter; remove from heat. Stir in 1/3 cup sugar and cocoa. Add gelatin mixture; blend well. Slightly beat egg yolks; stir into chocolate mixture. Cook over medium heat, stirring constantly, until mixture is hot and gelatin is dissolved. *Do not boil.* Remove from heat; stir in creme de cacao. Cool to room temperature, stirring occasionally. In large mixer bowl beat egg whites until foamy; gradually add remaining 1/3 cup sugar, beating until stiff peaks form. Fold in chocolate mixture; pour into pastry shell. Cover; chill about 4 hours or until set. *8 servings*

Creme de Cacao Pie

Hershey's Fudge Pie

- 3 1/2 cups (8-ounce container) frozen non-dairy whipped topping, thawed
- 1 cup HERSHEY'S Chocolate Fudge Topping, at room temperature
- 8-inch (6 ounces) packaged chocolate flavored crumb crust

In medium bowl stir together whipped topping and fudge topping until completely blended. Spoon into crust. Cover; chill or freeze until firm. Serve chilled or frozen.

6 to 8 servings

Peanut Butter Cream Pie

- 1 package (3 1/2 ounces) instant vanilla pudding and pie filling
- 1 cup dairy sour cream
- 1 cup milk
- 1 1/2 cups REESE'S Peanut Butter Chips
- 2 tablespoons vegetable oil
- 8-inch (6 ounces) packaged crumb crust
- Whipped topping

In small mixer bowl blend pudding mix, sour cream and milk; set aside. In top of double boiler over hot, not boiling, water melt peanut butter chips with oil, stirring constantly to blend. (OR in small microwave-safe bowl place chips and oil. Microwave at HIGH (100%) 45 seconds; stir. If necessary, microwave at HIGH additional 15 seconds or until melted and smooth when stirred.) Gradually add to pudding, blending well. Pour into crust. Cover; chill several hours or overnight. Garnish with whipped topping. *6 to 8 servings*

Chocolate Mousse Pie with Rum Cream Topping

Chocolate Mousse (recipe page 68)
8-inch baked pastry shell or 8-inch (6 ounces) packaged chocolate flavored crumb crust
1 cup chilled whipping cream
2 tablespoons confectioners' sugar
2 teaspoons light rum or 1/4 teaspoon rum extract

Prepare Chocolate Mousse. Pour mixture into pastry shell. In small mixer bowl beat cream, confectioners' sugar and rum until stiff. Spread topping over mousse. Cover; chill at least 2 hours. Garnish as desired. *6 to 8 servings*

Chocolate Cream Pie

1 package (3 ounces) cream cheese, softened
1/2 cup sugar
1 teaspoon vanilla extract
1/3 cup HERSHEY'S Cocoa
1/3 cup milk
1 container (8 ounces) frozen non-dairy whipped topping, thawed
8-inch (6 ounces) packaged graham crumb crust

In small mixer bowl combine cream cheese, sugar and vanilla until blended. Add cocoa alternately with milk, beating until smooth. Gradually fold in whipped topping until well combined. Spoon into pie shell. Cover; chill 4 to 6 hours or until set.
6 to 8 servings

Chocolate Mousse Pie with Rum Cream Topping

Chocolatetown Pie

9-inch unbaked pastry shell
1/2 cup butter or margarine, softened
2 eggs, beaten
2 teaspoons vanilla extract or 2 tablespoons bourbon
1 cup sugar
1/2 cup all-purpose flour
1 cup HERSHEY'S Semi-Sweet Chocolate Chips or MINI CHIPS
1 cup chopped pecans or walnuts
Festive Whipped Cream (optional, recipe follows)

Prepare pastry shell; set aside. Heat oven to 350°. In small mixer bowl cream butter; add eggs and vanilla. Combine sugar and flour; add to creamed mixture. Stir in chocolate chips and nuts; pour into unbaked pastry shell. Bake 45 to 50 minutes or until golden. Cool about 1 hour; serve warm. Serve with Festive Whipped Cream, if desired. Garnish as desired. *8 to 10 servings*

Festive Whipped Cream

1/2 cup chilled whipping cream
2 tablespoons confectioners' sugar
1/4 teaspoon vanilla extract or 1 teaspoon bourbon

In small mixer bowl combine all ingredients; beat until stiff.
About 1 cup topping

Meringue Topped Chocolate Cream Pie

9-inch baked pastry shell
1 cup sugar
1/2 cup all-purpose flour
6 tablespoons HERSHEY'S Cocoa
1/2 teaspoon salt
2 cups milk
3 egg yolks, slightly beaten
1/4 cup butter or margarine
2 teaspoons vanilla extract
Meringue Topping (recipe follows)

Prepare pastry shell; cool. In medium saucepan combine sugar, flour, cocoa and salt; stir in milk. Cook over medium heat, stirring constantly, until mixture boils; remove from heat. Stir half of mixture into beaten egg yolks; return mixture to saucepan. Continue cooking and stirring over medium heat until mixture boils; boil and stir 1 minute. Remove from heat; stir in butter and vanilla. Press plastic wrap directly onto surface. Cool 10 minutes; pour into baked pastry shell. Heat oven to 350°. Meanwhile, prepare Meringue Topping; spread over warm filling, carefully sealing to edges of crust. Bake 5 to 8 minutes or just until meringue is lightly browned. Cool to room temperature; chill several hours. Refrigerate leftovers.

8 servings

Meringue Topping

In small mixer bowl beat 4 egg whites and 1/2 teaspoon cream of tartar until foamy. Gradually add 6 tablespoons sugar; beat until stiff peaks form and sugar is dissolved.

Chocolate Eggnog Pie

Chocolate Crumb Crust (recipe follows)
1 envelope unflavored gelatin
3/4 cup granulated sugar, divided
1/3 cup HERSHEY'S Cocoa
1/8 teaspoon salt
3 eggs, separated
1 1/4 cups milk
2 tablespoons rum or 3/4 teaspoon rum extract
1/2 teaspoon vanilla extract
1/4 teaspoon ground nutmeg
1 cup chilled whipping cream, divided
2 tablespoons confectioners' sugar
Ground nutmeg (optional)

Prepare Chocolate Crumb Crust; set aside. In medium saucepan stir together gelatin, 1/2 cup granulated sugar, cocoa and salt; stir in egg yolks beaten with milk. Let stand 5 minutes. Cook over low heat, stirring constantly, until gelatin is completely dissolved and mixture thickens slightly, about 5 minutes. *Do not boil.* Remove from heat; stir in rum, vanilla and 1/4 teaspoon nutmeg. Pour mixture into large bowl; chill, stirring occasionally, until mixture mounds slightly when dropped from spoon. In small mixer bowl beat egg whites until foamy. Add remaining 1/4 cup granulated sugar, 1 tablespoon at a time, beating until stiff peaks form; fold into chocolate mixture. In small bowl beat 1/2 cup whipping cream until stiff; fold into chocolate mixture. Chill 10 minutes. Spoon mixture into cooled crust; chill until firm, about 4 hours. Beat remaining 1/2 cup whipping cream and confectioners' sugar until stiff; spoon around edge of pie. Sprinkle ground nutmeg over whipped cream, if desired.

8 servings

Chocolate Crumb Crust

Heat oven to 350°. In medium bowl stir together 1 1/2 cups vanilla wafer crumbs (about 45 wafers), 1/3 cup confectioners' sugar, 1/3 cup HERSHEY'S Cocoa and 6 tablespoons melted butter or margarine. Press crumb mixture onto bottom and up sides of 9-inch pie plate. Bake 8 minutes. Cool on wire rack before filling.

Smooth-n-Rich Chocolate Pie

1 cup confectioners' sugar
1/2 cup butter, softened
5 squares (5 ounces) HERSHEY'S Semi-Sweet Baking Chocolate, melted and cooled
1 teaspoon vanilla extract
2 eggs
1/2 cup chilled whipping cream
8-inch (6 ounces) packaged graham cracker crumb crust

In small mixer bowl combine confectioners' sugar and butter; beat until light and fluffy. Blend in cooled chocolate and vanilla; beat in eggs. In separate bowl beat whipping cream until stiff; fold into chocolate mixture. Spoon into crust. Cover; freeze until firm.

6 to 8 servings

BREADS, MUFFINS & COFFEECAKES

Let the irresistible aroma of these breads and coffeecakes fill your kitchen.

Chocolate Chip Banana Bread (top) and Quick Cocoa-Bran Muffins (recipes page 102)

Chocolate Chip Banana Bread

- 2 cups all-purpose flour
- 1 cup sugar
- 1 teaspoon baking powder
- 1/2 teaspoon baking soda
- 1 teaspoon salt
- 1 cup mashed ripe bananas (about 3 small)
- 1/2 cup shortening
- 2 eggs
- 1 cup HERSHEY'S Semi-Sweet Chocolate Chips
- 1/2 cup chopped walnuts

Heat oven to 350°. Grease bottoms only of two 8 1/2 x 4 1/2 x 2 1/2-inch loaf pans. In large mixer bowl combine all ingredients except chocolate chips and walnuts; blend well on medium speed. Stir in chips and walnuts. Pour into prepared pans. Bake 45 to 50 minutes or until wooden pick inserted in center comes out clean. Cool 10 minutes; remove from pans. Cool completely on wire rack. *2 loaves*

Quick Cocoa-Bran Muffins

- 1 package (10.75 ounces) bran and honey muffin mix
- 1/4 cup HERSHEY'S Cocoa
- 1 egg, slightly beaten
- 3/4 cup water
- 1/2 cup raisins
- 1/2 cup finely chopped nuts (optional)

Heat oven to 400°. Grease or paper-line 12 muffin cups (2 1/2 inches in diameter). In large bowl combine muffin mix and cocoa. Stir in egg and water just until blended. Stir in raisins and nuts, if desired. Fill muffin cups 3/4 full with batter. Bake 15 to 17 minutes or until wooden pick inserted in center comes out clean. Serve warm. *About 1 dozen muffins*

Chocolate Almond Braided Coffeecake

- 1/3 cup HERSHEY'S Semi-Sweet Chocolate Chips, melted and cooled
- 1/3 cup sugar
- 1/4 cup dairy sour cream
- 2 tablespoons chopped, toasted almonds*
- 1 can (8 ounces) refrigerated quick crescent dinner rolls

Heat oven to 350°. In small mixer bowl combine melted chocolate, sugar and sour cream; stir in almonds. On ungreased cookie sheet unroll dough into 2 long rectangles. Overlap long sides to form 13 x 7-inch rectangle; press perforations to seal. Spread chocolate mixture in 2-inch strip lengthwise down center of dough. Make cuts 1 inch apart on each side just to edge of filling. Fold strips at an angle across filling, alternating from side to side. Fold under ends to seal. Bake 20 to 25 minutes or until browned. Cool; cut into slices. Serve warm. *8 servings*

*To toast almonds: Toast in shallow baking pan in 350° oven, stirring occasionally, 8 to 10 minutes or until golden brown.

Chocolate Dessert Waffles

- 1/2 cup HERSHEY'S Cocoa
- 1/4 cup butter or margarine, melted
- 3/4 cup sugar
- 2 eggs
- 2 teaspoons vanilla extract
- 1 cup all-purpose flour
- 1/2 teaspoon baking soda
- 1/2 teaspoon salt
- 1/2 cup buttermilk or sour milk*
- 1/2 cup chopped nuts (optional)
- Hot Fudge Sauce (recipe page 93)
- Strawberry Dessert Cream (recipe follows)

In small mixer bowl blend cocoa and butter until smooth; stir in sugar. Add eggs and vanilla; beat well. Combine flour, baking soda and salt; add alternately with buttermilk to cocoa mixture. Stir in nuts, if desired. Bake in waffle iron according to manufacturer's directions. Carefully remove waffle from iron. Serve warm with Hot Fudge Sauce and Strawberry Dessert Cream.

About ten 4-inch waffles

*To sour milk: Use 1 1/2 teaspoons white vinegar plus milk to equal 1/2 cup.

Strawberry Dessert Cream

In small mixer bowl beat 1 cup chilled whipping cream until stiff. Fold in 1/3 cup strawberry preserves and 3 drops red food color, if desired.

About 2 cups topping

Chocolate Sticky Bubble Loaf

- 2 loaves frozen bread dough, thawed
- 3/4 cup sugar
- 4 tablespoons HERSHEY'S Cocoa, divided
- 1 teaspoon ground cinnamon
- 1/2 cup butter or margarine, melted and divided
- 1/4 cup water
- 1/2 cup packed light brown sugar
- 1/2 cup pecan pieces

Thaw loaves as directed on package; let rise until doubled. In small bowl combine sugar, 1 tablespoon cocoa and cinnamon; set aside. In small microwave-safe bowl combine 1/4 cup melted butter, water, brown sugar and remaining 3 tablespoons cocoa; microwave at HIGH (100%) 30 to 60 seconds or until smooth when stirred. Pour mixture into 12-cup Bundt pan; sprinkle with pecan pieces. Heat oven to 350°. Pinch off pieces of bread dough; form into balls, 1 1/2 inches in diameter. Dip each in remaining 1/4 cup melted butter and roll in cocoa-sugar mixture. Place balls in prepared pan. Bake 45 to 50 minutes or until golden brown. Cool 10 minutes in pan; invert onto serving plate. Serve warm or cool.

12 servings

Chocolate Upside Down Coffeecake

- 3/4 cup apple jelly
- 1 package (16 ounces) pound cake mix
- 1 cup HERSHEY'S Milk Chocolate Chips, divided

Heat oven to 325°. Grease and flour 9-inch square baking pan. Spread jelly evenly onto bottom of prepared pan. Prepare cake batter according to package directions. Stir in 1/2 cup milk chocolate chips. Pour batter over jelly layer, spreading gently and evenly. Sprinkle remaining 1/2 cup chips over top. Bake 50 to 55 minutes or until cake springs back when touched lightly. Cool 5 minutes in pan; invert onto serving plate. Cool at least 15 minutes; serve warm.

About 9 servings

Cocoa-Nut Bread

- 2 1/4 cups all-purpose flour
- 1 1/2 cups sugar
- 1/3 cup HERSHEY'S Cocoa
- 3 1/2 teaspoons baking powder
- 1 teaspoon salt
- 1 egg
- 1 1/4 cups milk
- 1/2 cup vegetable oil
- 1 cup finely chopped nuts

Heat oven to 350°. Grease and flour 9 x 5 x 3-inch loaf pan. In large bowl combine all ingredients except nuts. Beat with spoon 30 seconds; stir in nuts. Pour into prepared pan. Bake 65 to 70 minutes or until wooden pick inserted in center comes out clean. Cool 10 minutes; remove from pan. Wrap tightly in foil. Cool completely.

1 loaf

Mini Chips Cinnamon Crescents

Mini Chips Cinnamon Crescents

- 1 can (8 ounces) refrigerated quick crescent dinner rolls
- Ground cinnamon
- 1/2 cup HERSHEY'S MINI CHIPS Semi-Sweet Chocolate
- Confectioners' sugar

Heat oven to 375°. On ungreased cookie sheet unroll dough to form 8 triangles. Lightly sprinkle cinnamon and 1 tablespoon MINI CHIPS Chocolate on top of each. Gently press into dough to adhere. Starting at shortest side of triangle, roll dough to opposite point. Bake 10 to 12 minutes or until golden brown. Sprinkle confectioners' sugar over top. Serve warm.

8 crescents

Mini Chips Blueberry Bread

- 2 packages (14.5 ounces each) blueberry nut quick bread mix
- 2 eggs, slightly beaten
- 3/4 cup buttermilk or sour milk*
- 1/2 cup vegetable oil
- 1 1/2 cups HERSHEY'S MINI CHIPS Semi-Sweet Chocolate
- MINI CHIPS Glaze (recipe follows)

Heat oven to 350°. Grease and flour 12-cup Bundt pan. In large bowl combine bread mix, eggs, buttermilk and oil. Beat with spoon 1 minute. Stir in MINI CHIPS Chocolate. Pour into prepared pan. Bake 45 to 50 minutes or until wooden pick inserted in center comes out clean. Cool 10 minutes; remove from pan. Wrap tightly in foil. Cool completely. Glaze with MINI CHIPS Glaze.

12 servings

*To sour milk: Use 2 teaspoons white vinegar plus milk to equal 3/4 cup.

Loaf Version: Prepare half of batter as directed above using 1 package blueberry nut quick bread mix, 1 egg, 6 tablespoons buttermilk or sour milk, 1/4 cup vegetable oil and 3/4 cup MINI CHIPS Semi-Sweet Chocolate. Pour batter into greased and floured 9 x 5 x 3-inch loaf pan. Bake; cool as directed above.

1 loaf

MINI CHIPS Glaze

In small saucepan bring 2 tablespoons sugar and 2 tablespoons water to boil, stirring until sugar dissolves. Remove from heat; add 1/2 cup HERSHEY'S MINI CHIPS Semi-Sweet Chocolate. Stir with wire whisk until chips are melted and mixture is smooth; use immediately.

About 1/2 cup glaze

Mini Chips Blueberry Breakfast Cake

- 1 package (14.5 ounces) blueberry nut quick bread mix
- 1 cup dairy sour cream
- 1/4 cup water
- 1 egg
- 1/2 cup HERSHEY'S MINI CHIPS Semi-Sweet Chocolate
- Topping (recipe follows)

Heat oven to 350°. Grease bottom only of 9-inch square baking pan. In medium bowl combine bread mix, sour cream, water, egg and MINI CHIPS Chocolate; stir until well moistened and blended. Spread into prepared pan. Sprinkle Topping over batter. Bake 40 to 45 minutes or until golden brown. Cool; cut into squares.

9 servings

Topping

In small bowl combine 1/4 cup all-purpose flour, 1/4 cup sugar and 2 tablespoons softened butter or margarine until crumbly. Stir in 1/4 cup MINI CHIPS Chocolate.

Mini Chips Blueberry Bread (top) and Mini Chips Blueberry Breakfast Cake

Mini Chips Surprise Muffins

- 1 package (16.1 ounces) nut quick bread mix
- 1 egg, slightly beaten
- 1 cup milk
- 1/4 cup vegetable oil
- 1 cup HERSHEY'S MINI CHIPS Semi-Sweet Chocolate
- 1/3 cup fruit preserves, any flavor

Heat oven to 400°. Grease or paper-line 18 muffin cups (2 1/2 inches in diameter). In large bowl combine bread mix, egg, milk and oil. Beat with spoon 1 minute. Stir in MINI CHIPS Chocolate. Fill muffin cups 1/4 full with batter. Spoon 1/2 teaspoon preserves onto center of batter. Fill muffin cups 3/4 full with batter. Bake 20 to 22 minutes or until lightly browned. Serve warm.

About 1 1/2 dozen muffins

Mini Chips Surprise Muffins

Black Forest Crepes

- 3 eggs
- 1 cup all-purpose flour
- 2 tablespoons HERSHEY'S Cocoa
- 2 tablespoons sugar
- 1 1/4 cups buttermilk or sour milk*
- 3 tablespoons butter, melted
- Additional melted butter
- Cherry pie filling
- Sweetened whipped cream
- Chocolate Sauce (recipe follows)

In small mixer bowl beat eggs. Combine flour, cocoa and sugar; add to eggs alternately with buttermilk, beating until smooth. Beat in 3 tablespoons butter; chill about 1 hour. Heat small skillet or crepe pan (7-inch diameter) over medium heat; brush lightly with melted butter. For each crepe, pour about 2 tablespoons batter in pan; immediately rotate pan to evenly cover bottom. Cook until crepe surface begins to dry, about 1 minute; turn and cook other side. Stack crepes, placing wax paper between each. (Refrigerate or freeze for later use, if desired.) Just before serving, place 2 tablespoons pie filling in center of each crepe; fold edges over filling. Place in shallow oven-proof dish; heat in oven at 225° for 15 minutes.** Drizzle with Chocolate Sauce; top with sweetened whipped cream.

About 18 crepes

*To sour milk: Use 4 teaspoons white vinegar plus milk to equal 1 1/4 cups.

****Microwave Heating Directions:** Place 8 filled crepes in shallow microwave-safe dish. Microwave at HIGH (100%) 1 to 1 1/2 minutes, or just until crepes are warm.

Chocolate Sauce

3/4 cup sugar
1/3 cup HERSHEY'S Cocoa
3/4 cup evaporated milk
1/4 cup butter or margarine
1/8 teaspoon salt
1 teaspoon kirsch (optional)

In small saucepan combine sugar and cocoa; blend in evaporated milk, butter and salt. Cook over medium heat, stirring constantly, until mixture boils. Remove from heat; stir in kirsch, if desired. Serve warm. Store leftover sauce, covered, in refrigerator. *About 1 cup sauce*

Cocoa-Cinnamon Toast

1/4 cup sugar
1 tablespoon HERSHEY'S Cocoa
2 teaspoons ground cinnamon
Bread slices
Butter or margarine, softened

In small bowl combine sugar, cocoa and cinnamon; set aside. On cookie sheet place desired number bread slices. Broil about 5 inches from heat 1 minute or until golden brown; remove from oven. Turn slices over so untoasted sides face up. Place about 2 teaspoons butter on each slice; spread evenly. Sprinkle each buttered slice with about 1 teaspoon cocoa-cinnamon mixture. Return to oven; broil about 5 inches from heat 1 minute or just until bubbly. (Watch carefully.) Serve warm.

About 16 slices toast

Note: Cocoa-cinnamon mixture can be covered and stored for later use.

Chocolate Chip Fruit Muffins

Chocolate Chip Fruit Muffins

1 package (15 ounces) banana quick bread mix
2 eggs, slightly beaten
1 cup milk
1/4 cup vegetable oil
1 cup HERSHEY'S Semi-Sweet Chocolate Chips, MINI CHIPS or Milk Chocolate Chips
1/2 cup dried fruit bits

Heat oven to 400°. Grease or paper-line 18 muffin cups (2 1/2 inches in diameter). In large bowl combine bread mix, eggs, milk and oil. Beat with spoon 30 seconds. Stir in chocolate chips and fruit bits. Fill muffin cups 3/4 full with batter. Bake 18 to 20 minutes or until lightly browned. Serve warm.

About 1 1/2 dozen muffins

Chocolate Streusel & Spice Coffeecake

- 1 package (10 to 13 ounces) fruit, cinnamon, spice or bran muffin mix
- 1/2 cup HERSHEY'S Semi-Sweet Chocolate Chips
- 3/4 cup confectioners' sugar
- 1/2 cup chopped nuts
- 1/4 cup HERSHEY'S Cocoa
- 3 tablespoons butter or margarine, melted

Heat oven to 350°. Grease bottom only of 9-inch square baking pan. Prepare muffin mix as directed; stir in chocolate chips. Pour into prepared pan. In small bowl combine confectioners' sugar, nuts and cocoa; with fork stir in butter until crumbly. Sprinkle over batter. Bake 25 to 30 minutes or until wooden pick inserted in center comes out clean. Cool.

9 servings

Easy Chocolate Zucchini Cake

- 1 package (16.1 ounces) nut quick bread mix
- 1/2 cup sugar
- 1 teaspoon ground cinnamon
- 3/4 cup vegetable oil
- 3 eggs, slightly beaten
- 1 1/2 cups shredded zucchini
- 1 cup HERSHEY'S Semi-Sweet Chocolate Chips
- Confectioners' sugar (optional)

Heat oven to 350°. Grease and flour 9-inch square baking pan. In large bowl combine bread mix, sugar, cinnamon, oil and eggs; mix until well blended. Stir in zucchini and chocolate chips; pour into prepared pan. Bake 40 to 45 minutes or until wooden pick inserted in center comes out clean. Cool. Sprinkle confectioners' sugar over top, if desired. Cover; refrigerate leftovers.

9 servings

Chocolate Streusel & Spice Coffeecake

Chocolate Quickie Stickies

- 6 tablespoons butter or margarine
- $\frac{3}{4}$ cup packed light brown sugar
- 4 tablespoons HERSHEY'S Cocoa, divided
- 5 teaspoons water
- 1 teaspoon vanilla extract
- $\frac{1}{2}$ cup coarsely chopped nuts (optional)
- 2 cans (8 ounces each) refrigerated quick crescent dinner rolls
- $2\frac{1}{2}$ tablespoons butter or margarine, softened
- 2 tablespoons granulated sugar

Heat oven to 350°. In small saucepan over low heat melt 6 tablespoons butter. Add brown sugar, 3 tablespoons cocoa and water. Cook over medium heat, stirring constantly, just until mixture comes to boil. Remove from heat; add vanilla.

Chocolate Quickie Stickies

Spoon about 1 teaspoonful chocolate mixture into each of 48 small muffin cups ($1\frac{3}{4}$ inches in diameter). Sprinkle $\frac{1}{2}$ teaspoon nuts, if desired, into each cup; set aside. Separate rolls into 8 rectangles; firmly press diagonal perforations to seal. Combine softened butter, granulated sugar and remaining 1 tablespoon cocoa; evenly spread thin layer over each rectangle. Starting at longer side, roll up. Pinch seams to seal. Cut each roll into 6 equal pieces. Place in prepared pans, cut side down. Bake 11 to 13 minutes or until light brown. Remove from oven; cool 30 seconds. Invert onto cookie sheet. Let stand 1 minute; remove pan. Serve warm or cool. *4 dozen small rolls*

Note: Rolls can be baked in two $8 \times 1\frac{1}{2}$-inch round pans. Heat oven to 350°. Cook chocolate mixture as directed; place $\frac{1}{2}$ in each pan. Prepare rolls as directed; place 24 pieces, cut side down, in each pan. Bake 20 to 22 minutes. Cool and remove from pan as above.

Easy Chocolate Zucchini Cake

Cocoa Applesauce Muffins

- Cocoa Crunch Topping (optional, recipe follows)
- 1/4 cup HERSHEY'S Cocoa
- 1/4 cup vegetable oil
- 3/4 cup chunky applesauce
- 1 egg, beaten
- 1 1/4 cups all-purpose flour
- 3/4 cup sugar
- 3/4 teaspoon baking soda
- 1/4 teaspoon salt
- 1/8 teaspoon ground cinnamon
- 1/2 cup chopped nuts

Heat oven to 400°. Grease bottoms only of 12 muffin cups (2 1/2 inches in diameter). Prepare Cocoa Crunch Topping, if desired; set aside. In small bowl combine cocoa and oil; stir until smooth. Add applesauce and egg; blend well. In medium bowl combine flour, sugar, baking soda, salt and cinnamon; stir in applesauce mixture and nuts, blending just until dry ingredients are moistened. Fill muffin cups about 2/3 full. Sprinkle heaping teaspoonful Topping on each muffin, if desired. Bake 20 to 25 minutes or until wooden pick inserted in center comes out clean. Let cool about 5 minutes. Remove from pan; serve warm.

About 1 dozen muffins

Cocoa Crunch Topping

- 1/4 cup packed light brown sugar
- 1/4 cup chopped nuts (optional)
- 2 tablespoons butter or margarine
- 2 tablespoons HERSHEY'S Cocoa
- 2 tablespoons all-purpose flour

In small bowl combine all ingredients until crumbly. (Leftover topping can be stored in covered container in refrigerator.)

Chocolate Chip Crater Cake

- 2 cups all-purpose biscuit baking mix
- 1/4 cup sugar
- 2/3 cup milk
- 1 egg
- 1 teaspoon vanilla extract
- 1 cup HERSHEY'S Semi-Sweet Chocolate Chips
- Topping Mix (recipe follows)

Heat oven to 350°. Grease 8-inch square baking pan. In large mixer bowl combine biscuit mix, sugar, milk, egg and vanilla; beat on low speed until moistened. Beat 2 minutes on medium speed until smooth. Pour 1/2 of batter into prepared pan. Sprinkle chocolate chips over batter. Top with remaining batter, completely covering chips. Sprinkle Topping Mix evenly over batter. Bake 25 to 30 minutes or until top springs back when touched lightly. Cool completely.

About 9 servings

Topping Mix

- 1/4 cup granulated sugar
- 1/4 cup packed dark brown sugar
- 1/4 cup packaged all-purpose biscuit baking mix
- 1/4 cup butter or margarine, softened
- 1 teaspoon ground cinnamon

In small bowl combine all ingredients.

Cinnamon Chip Muffins

2 cups all-purpose biscuit baking mix
1/4 cup sugar
1 egg
2/3 cup milk
1 cup HERSHEY'S MINI CHIPS Semi-Sweet Chocolate
1/4 cup finely chopped nuts (optional)
Sugar-Cinnamon Topping (recipe follows)

Heat oven to 400°. Grease or paper-line 12 muffin cups (2 1/2 inches in diameter). In large bowl combine baking mix, sugar, egg and milk. Beat with spoon 30 seconds. Stir in MINI CHIPS Chocolate and nuts, if desired. Fill muffin cups 3/4 full with batter. Sprinkle each with about 1/2 teaspoon Sugar-Cinnamon Topping. Bake 15 to 17 minutes or until very lightly browned. Serve warm.

About 1 dozen muffins

Sugar-Cinnamon Topping

In small bowl combine 2 tablespoons sugar and 2 teaspoons ground cinnamon.

Glazed Chocolate Buttermilk Doughnuts

2 eggs
1 1/4 cups sugar
1/2 teaspoon vegetable oil
1 teaspoon vanilla extract
4 cups all-purpose flour
1/3 cup HERSHEY'S Cocoa
1 tablespoon plus 1 teaspoon baking powder
1 teaspoon ground cinnamon
3/4 teaspoon salt
1/4 teaspoon baking soda
3/4 cup buttermilk
Vegetable oil
Chocolate Glaze (recipe follows)
Chopped nuts or flaked coconut (optional)

In large mixer bowl beat eggs well. Gradually add sugar, beating until thick and light in color. Add oil and vanilla. Stir together flour, cocoa, baking powder, cinnamon, salt and baking soda; add to egg mixture alternately with buttermilk, beginning and ending with flour mixture. Cover; chill several hours. Divide dough in half. Working with 1 portion at a time, place dough on lightly floured surface; roll out to 1/2-inch thickness. Cut dough with floured 2 1/2-inch doughnut cutter. Heat 2 inches oil in fry pan or deep fryer to 375°. Fry doughnuts in hot oil about 2 minutes, turning once during frying. Drain on paper towels. Dip top of each doughnut in Chocolate Glaze. Garnish with nuts or coconut, if desired.

About 2 dozen doughnuts

Mini Chips Pancakes

Chocolate Glaze

1 tablespoon butter or margarine
1 1/2 tablespoons HERSHEY'S Cocoa
2 tablespoons water
1 cup confectioners' sugar
1/4 teaspoon vanilla extract

In small saucepan over low heat melt butter; add cocoa and water, stirring constantly until mixture thickens. *Do not boil*. Remove from heat; gradually add confectioners' sugar and vanilla, beating with wire whisk until smooth. Add additional water, 1/2 teaspoon at a time, until glaze is desired consistency.

About 3/4 cup glaze

Mini Chips Pancakes

1 carton (16 ounces) frozen pancake batter, thawed
1/2 cup HERSHEY'S MINI CHIPS Semi-Sweet Chocolate
Fruit syrup or pancake syrup

Lightly grease griddle; heat to 375°. In small bowl combine pancake batter and MINI CHIPS Chocolate. Pour about 2 tablespoons batter onto hot griddle. Turn when surface is bubbly; cook until lightly browned. Serve warm with syrup.

About 14 four-inch pancakes

CANDIES & SNACKS

Easiest-ever candies for holiday gift giving, plus plenty of great treats for anytime snacking.

Clockwise from far left: Easy Rocky Road, Pastel-Coated Cocoa Bonbons, Easy Double Decker Fudge (recipes page 118) and Coconut Honey Bars (recipe 119).

Easy Rocky Road

- 2 cups (12-ounce package) HERSHEY'S Semi-Sweet Chocolate Chips
- 1/4 cup butter or margarine
- 2 tablespoons shortening
- 3 cups miniature marshmallows
- 1/2 cup coarsely chopped nuts

Microwave Directions: Butter 8-inch square pan. In large microwave-safe bowl place chocolate chips, butter and shortening; microwave at MEDIUM (50%) 5 to 7 minutes or until chips are melted and mixture is smooth when stirred. Add marshmallows and nuts; blend well. Spread evenly into prepared pan. Cover; chill until firm. Cut into 2-inch squares. *16 squares*

Pastel-Coated Cocoa Bonbons

- 2 packages (3 ounces each) cream cheese, softened
- 2 cups confectioners' sugar
- 1/2 cup HERSHEY'S Cocoa
- 2 tablespoons butter, melted
- 1 teaspoon vanilla extract
- Pastel Coating (recipe follows)

In small mixer bowl beat cream cheese. Add confectioners' sugar, cocoa, butter and vanilla; blend well. Cover; chill several hours or until firm enough to handle. Shape into 1-inch balls; place on wax paper-covered tray. Refrigerate, uncovered, 3 to 4 hours or until dry. Using long fork dip cold centers into very warm Pastel Coating. Quickly remove. Place on wax paper-covered tray; swirl coating on top of bonbon. Refrigerate until firm. Store in airtight container in refrigerator.

2 dozen bonbons

Pastel Coating

- 6 tablespoons butter
- 3 cups confectioners' sugar
- 1/4 cup milk
- 1 teaspoon vanilla extract
- Red or green food color

In medium microwave-safe bowl combine all ingredients except food color. Microwave at HIGH (100%) 1 to 1 1/2 minutes or until smooth when stirred. Tint pastel pink or green with several drops food color.

Easy Double Decker Fudge

- 2 cups (12-ounce package) REESE'S Peanut Butter Chips
- 2 cups (12-ounce package) HERSHEY'S Semi-Sweet Chocolate Chips
- 2 cans (14-ounces each) sweetened condensed milk, divided
- 3 tablespoons butter

Microwave Directions: Line 13×9×2-inch pan with foil. Place peanut butter chips and chocolate chips in two separate medium microwave-safe bowls. Pour 1 can sweetened condensed milk into each bowl. Microwave bowl with peanut butter chips at HIGH (100%) 1 1/2 to 2 minutes or until chips are melted and mixture is smooth when stirred; stir in butter. Immediately pour and spread into prepared pan. Microwave bowl with chocolate chips at HIGH 1 1/2 to 2 minutes or until chips are melted and mixture is smooth when stirred. Immediately pour and spread over peanut butter layer. Cool. Cover; chill until firm. Cut into 1-inch squares.

About 8 dozen squares

Chocolate Marshmallow Slices

Coconut Honey Bars

- 1/3 cup butter or margarine
- 1/3 cup packed light brown sugar
- 1/3 cup honey
- 1/2 teaspoon vanilla extract
- 2 cups quick-cooking rolled oats
- 1 1/3 cups flaked coconut
- 1/2 cup raisins
- 1 cup REESE'S Peanut Butter Chips or HERSHEY'S Semi-Sweet Chocolate Chips

Heat oven to 400°. Grease 8-inch square baking pan. In large saucepan melt butter; remove from heat. Add remaining ingredients; stir until blended. Press mixture into prepared pan. Bake 15 to 20 minutes or just until golden brown. Cool completely; cut into bars.

About 2 dozen bars

Chocolate Marshmallow Slices

- 2 cups (12-ounce package) HERSHEY'S Semi-Sweet Chocolate Chips
- 1/2 cup butter or margarine
- 6 cups (10 1/2 ounce package) miniature marshmallows
- 1 cup finely chopped nuts
- Additional chopped nuts

In medium saucepan over low heat melt chocolate chips and butter, stirring constantly until blended. Remove from heat; cool 5 minutes. Stir in marshmallows and 1 cup nuts; *do not melt marshmallows.* On wax paper shape mixture into 2 rolls, 2 inches in diameter. Wrap in foil; chill 15 minutes. Roll in additional chopped nuts. Wrap; chill overnight. Cut rolls into 1/4-inch slices. Store in airtight container in cool, dry place.

About 3 dozen slices

Chocolate-Peanut Butter Clusters

- 1/2 cup HERSHEY'S Milk Chocolate Chips
- 1/2 cup HERSHEY'S Semi-Sweet Chocolate Chips
- 1 tablespoon shortening
- 1 cup unsalted, roasted peanuts

Microwave Directions: In small microwave-safe bowl place milk chocolate chips, semi-sweet chocolate chips and shortening. Microwave at HIGH (100%) 1 to 1 1/2 minutes or just until chips are melted and mixture is smooth when stirred. Stir in peanuts. Drop by teaspoonfuls into 1-inch diameter candy or petit four papers. Allow to set until firm. Store in airtight container in cool, dry place. *About 2 dozen clusters*

Chocolate Dipped Snacks

Chocolate Dipped Snacks

- 1/2 cup HERSHEY'S Milk Chocolate Chips
- 1/2 cup HERSHEY'S Semi-Sweet Chocolate Chips
- 1 tablespoon shortening
- Potato chips, cookies, dried apricots or miniature pretzels

Microwave Directions: In small microwave-safe bowl place milk chocolate chips, semi-sweet chocolate chips and shortening. Microwave at HIGH (100%) 1 to 1 1/2 minutes or just until chips are melted and mixture is smooth when stirred. Cool slightly. Dip 2/3 of each snack or fruit into chocolate mixture. Shake gently to remove excess chocolate. Place on wax paper-covered tray. Chill, uncovered, about 30 minutes or until chocolate is firm. Store in airtight container in cool, dry place.

About 1/2 cup coating

Cocoa Fruit Balls

2 1/2 cups (about 12 ounces) mixed dried fruits (prunes, pears, apricots and apples)
1 1/4 cups (8 ounces) Mission figs
1 cup flaked coconut
2 tablespoons orange juice
2 tablespoons honey
1/2 cup HERSHEY'S Cocoa
Chopped nuts or confectioners' sugar

Remove pits from prunes and stems from figs, if necessary. Using metal blade of food processor, chop dried fruits, figs and coconut (or put through fine blade of food grinder). In large bowl combine orange juice, honey and cocoa with fruit-coconut mixture; mix well. Cover; chill thoroughly. Shape mixture into 1 1/4-inch balls. Roll in chopped nuts or confectioners' sugar. Store in airtight container at room temperature.

About 3 dozen balls

Chocolate Almond Logs

1 can (8 ounces) almond paste
2 cups vanilla wafer cookie crumbs (about 60 cookies, crushed)
1 1/3 cups confectioners' sugar
1 cup HERSHEY'S Cocoa
1 cup whipping cream
1 1/2 cups finely chopped almonds
Candied cherries, cut in half

In large bowl crumble almond paste with pastry blender. Combine vanilla wafer crumbs, confectioners' sugar and cocoa; add to almond paste. Stir in whipping cream; mix until well blended. Knead and shape mixture into smooth ball. Shape mixture into 2 rolls, 2 inches in diameter; roll in chopped almonds. Wrap in foil; chill until firm. Cut rolls into 1/4-inch slices; garnish with candied cherry halves. Store in airtight container in cool, dry place.

About 6 dozen slices

Note: Can be made entirely in food processor. Chop cookies and nuts separately; combine and add ingredients as directed.

Fast Chocolate-Pecan Fudge

½ cup butter or margarine
¾ cup HERSHEY'S Cocoa
4 cups confectioners' sugar
1 teaspoon vanilla extract
½ cup evaporated milk
1 cup pecan pieces
Pecan halves (optional)

Microwave Directions: Line 8-inch square pan with foil. In medium microwave-safe bowl place butter. Microwave at HIGH (100%) 1 to 1½ minutes or until melted. Add cocoa; stir until smooth. Stir in confectioners' sugar and vanilla; blend well (mixture will be dry and crumbly). Stir in evaporated milk. Microwave at HIGH 1 minute; stir. Microwave additional 1 minute or until mixture is hot. Beat with wooden spoon until smooth; add pecans. Pour into prepared pan. Cool. Cover; chill until firm. Cut into 1-inch squares. Garnish with pecan halves, if desired. Cover; store in refrigerator.

About 4 dozen squares

Conventional Directions: Prepare pan as above. In medium saucepan melt butter. Remove from heat; stir in cocoa. Stir in confectioners' sugar and vanilla; add evaporated milk. Stir constantly over low heat until warm and smooth; add pecan pieces. Pour into prepared pan; chill and store as above.

Mint 'n Chocolate Fudge

½ cup butter or margarine
¾ cup HERSHEY'S Cocoa
4 cups confectioners' sugar
1 teaspoon vanilla extract
½ cup evaporated milk
Pastel Mint Topping (recipe follows)

Microwave Directions: Line 8-inch square pan with foil. In medium microwave-safe bowl place butter. Microwave at HIGH (100%) 1 to 1½ minutes or until melted. Add cocoa; stir until smooth. Stir in confectioners' sugar and vanilla; blend well (mixture will be dry and crumbly). Stir in evaporated milk. Microwave at HIGH 1 to 2 minutes or until mixture is hot. Beat with wire whisk until smooth. Immediately pour into prepared pan. Cover; chill until firm. Spread Pastel Mint Topping evenly over fudge; chill until firm. Cut into 1-inch squares. Cover; store in refrigerator.

About 4 dozen squares

Pastel Mint Topping

In small mixer bowl beat 3 tablespoons softened butter or margarine, 1 tablespoon water and ⅛ to ¼ teaspoon mint extract until blended. Gradually add 1½ cups confectioners' sugar and 2 drops green or red food color. Beat until smooth.

From top to bottom: Cherries 'n Chocolate Fudge (recipe page 124), Fast Chocolate-Pecan Fudge and Mint 'n Chocolate Fudge

Cherries 'n Chocolate Fudge

- 1 can (14 ounces) sweetened condensed milk
- 2 cups (12-ounce package) HERSHEY'S Semi-Sweet Chocolate Chips
- 1/2 cup coarsely chopped almonds
- 1/2 cup chopped candied cherries
- 1 teaspoon almond extract
- Candied cherry halves (optional)

Line 8-inch square pan with foil. In medium microwave-safe bowl combine sweetened condensed milk and chocolate chips; stir lightly. Microwave at HIGH (100%) 1 1/2 to 2 minutes or until chips are melted and mixture is smooth when stirred. Stir in almonds, cherries and almond extract. Spread evenly in prepared pan. Cover; chill until firm. Cut into 1-inch squares. Garnish with cherry halves, if desired. Cover; store in refrigerator.

About 4 dozen squares

Chocolate-Peanut Butter Coated Apples

- 10 to 12 wooden ice cream sticks or skewers
- 10 to 12 medium apples, stems removed
- 2 cups (12-ounce package) REESE'S Peanut Butter Chips
- 2/3 cup HERSHEY'S Cocoa
- 2/3 cup confectioners' sugar
- 1/2 cup vegetable oil
- Chopped peanuts or flaked coconut (optional)

Chocolate-Peanut Butter Coated Apples

Insert wooden stick into each washed and thoroughly dried apple. In top of double boiler over hot, not boiling, water combine peanut butter chips, cocoa, confectioners' sugar and oil; stir constantly until chips are melted and mixture is smooth. Remove from heat. Dip apples in mixture; twirl to remove excess coating. (If coating becomes too thick, return to low heat or add additional oil, 1 teaspoon at a time.) Roll lower half of coated apple in peanuts or coconut, if desired. Allow to cool on wax paper-covered tray. Chill, if desired.

10 to 12 apples

Chocolate-Marshmallow Treats

Chocolate-Marshmallow Treats

2 cups (12-ounce package) HERSHEY'S Semi-Sweet Chocolate Chips
2 tablespoons shortening
12 large marshmallows
1 1/2 cups pecan halves

In top of double boiler over hot, not boiling, water melt chocolate chips and shortening, stirring until smooth. Remove from heat. Set aside; cool mixture to 85°F. Cut marshmallows in half horizontally; place on wax paper and flatten slightly. Set aside. To form base for treats make 24 clusters by arranging pecans on wax paper-covered tray in groups of five, placing flat side of pecan halves down and ends touching in center. Into center of each cluster of pecans spoon 1/2 teaspoon melted chocolate mixture. Use fork to dip marshmallow halves in melted mixture; place one half over each set of pecan clusters, pressing down slightly. Top with pecan half. Cool completely. Store, covered, in refrigerator. *2 dozen snacks*

Microwave Directions: In 1-quart microwave-safe bowl place chocolate chips and shortening. Microwave at HIGH (100%) 1 1/2 to 2 minutes, stirring once, until chips are melted and mixture is smooth when stirred. Proceed as above.

Mocha Truffles

- 1/4 cup whipping cream
- 3 tablespoons sugar
- 3 tablespoons butter
- 1 1/2 teaspoons powdered instant coffee
- 1/2 cup HERSHEY'S Semi-Sweet Chocolate Chips
- 1/2 teaspoon vanilla extract
- Chopped nuts or HERSHEY'S Semi-Sweet Baking Chocolate, grated

In small saucepan combine whipping cream, sugar, butter and instant coffee; cook over low heat, stirring constantly, just until mixture boils. Remove from heat; immediately add chocolate chips. Stir until chips are melted and mixture is smooth when stirred; add vanilla. Pour into small bowl; chill, stirring occasionally, until mixture begins to set. Cover; chill several hours or overnight to allow mixture to ripen and harden. Form small amounts of mixture into 1/2-inch balls, working quickly to prevent melting; roll in nuts or chocolate. Cover; store in refrigerator. Serve cold.

About 1 1/2 dozen truffles

Rich 'n Good Chocolate Truffles

- 1 2/3 cups whipping cream
- 1/2 cup butter or margarine
- 1 box (8 ounces) HERSHEY'S Semi-Sweet Baking Chocolate, broken into pieces and chopped*
- 1 1/3 cups HERSHEY'S Semi-Sweet Chocolate Chips, chopped*
- 1 tablespoon vanilla extract or desired liqueur
- Coating (recipe follows)

Rich 'n Good Chocolate Truffles (top) and Mocha Truffles

In medium saucepan combine whipping cream and butter. Cook over medium heat, stirring constantly, just until mixture boils; remove from heat. Stir in baking chocolate and chocolate chips until completely melted; continue stirring until mixture cools and thickens slightly. Stir in vanilla. Pour into shallow, glass dish. Cover; chill until firm. With spoon scoop mixture into 1-inch balls; roll in Coating. Cover; chill until firm. Reroll before serving, if desired. Serve cold.

About 4 dozen truffles

Coating

In small bowl combine 1/2 cup HERSHEY'S Cocoa, sifted, and 3 tablespoons confectioners' sugar, sifted.

*Food processor can be used for chopping chocolate.

Cocoa Party Mix

- **3 cups toasted oat cereal rings**
- **3 cups bite-size crispy wheat squares cereal**
- **2 cups salted peanuts**
- **2 cups miniature pretzels**
- **1 cup raisins**
- **1/2 cup butter or margarine, melted**
- **2 to 4 tablespoons HERSHEY'S Cocoa**
- **1/4 cup sugar**

Heat oven to 250°. In large bowl combine cereals, peanuts, pretzels and raisins. In small bowl blend butter, cocoa and sugar; stir into cereal mixture. Toss until ingredients are well coated. Pour mixture into 13×9×2-inch baking pan. Bake 1 hour, stirring every 15 minutes. Cool completely. Store in airtight container.

About 10 cups mix

Double Decker Fudge

- 2 cups (12-ounce package) REESE'S Peanut Butter Chips, divided
- 1/2 cup HERSHEY'S Cocoa
- 1/4 cup butter, melted
- 1 teaspoon vanilla extract
- 4 1/2 cups sugar
- 1 jar (7 ounces) marshmallow creme
- 1 1/2 cups (12-ounce can) evaporated milk
- 1/4 cup butter

Line 13 × 9 × 2-inch pan with aluminum foil. Place 1 cup peanut butter chips in medium bowl; set aside. In second medium bowl blend cocoa, melted butter and vanilla until mixture is smooth; add remaining 1 cup peanut butter chips. Set aside. In heavy 4-quart saucepan combine sugar, marshmallow creme, evaporated milk and 1/4 cup butter. Cook over medium heat, stirring constantly, until mixture comes to rolling boil; boil and stir 5 minutes. Remove from heat. Immediately add half of hot mixture to bowl with peanut butter chips only. Pour remainder into cocoa mixture; stir to blend. Beat peanut butter mixture until chips are completely melted; spread evenly in prepared pan. Beat cocoa mixture until chips are melted and mixture thickens. Spread evenly on top of peanut butter layer. Cool until firm. Remove from pan; peel off foil. Cut into squares. Store in airtight container in cool, dry place.

About 8 dozen squares

Chocolate Pralines

- 1 1/2 cups granulated sugar
- 1 1/2 cups packed light brown sugar
- 6 tablespoons HERSHEY'S Cocoa
- 1 cup light cream
- 6 tablespoons butter
- 1 teaspoon vanilla extract
- 2 cups coarsely broken pecans

Cover 2 cookie sheets with wax paper. In heavy 3-quart saucepan combine granulated sugar, brown sugar, cocoa and light cream. Cook over medium heat, stirring constantly, until mixture comes to full boil. Reduce heat to low; cook, stirring occasionally, to 234°F on a candy thermometer (soft-ball stage), or until syrup, when dropped into very cold water, forms soft ball that flattens when removed from water. (Bulb of candy thermometer should not rest on bottom of saucepan.) Remove from heat. Add butter and vanilla. *Do not stir.* Cool at room temperature to 160°F. Add pecans. Beat with wooden spoon just until mixture begins to thicken, *about 1 to 2 minutes,* but is still glossy. Quickly drop by teaspoonfuls onto prepared cookie sheets. Cool. Store tightly covered or wrap individually in plastic wrap.

About 3 dozen candies

Fudge Caramels

Fudge Caramels

- 2 cups sugar
- 2/3 cup HERSHEY'S Cocoa
- 1/8 teaspoon salt
- 1 cup light corn syrup
- 1 cup evaporated milk
- 1/2 cup water
- 1/4 cup butter or margarine
- 1 teaspoon vanilla extract

Butter 9-inch square pan; set aside. In heavy 3-quart saucepan combine sugar, cocoa, salt and corn syrup; stir in evaporated milk and water. Cook over medium heat, stirring constantly, until mixture boils. Cook, stirring frequently, to 245°F on a candy thermometer (firm-ball stage) or until syrup, when dropped into very cold water, forms a firm ball that does not flatten when removed from water. Remove from heat; stir in butter and vanilla, blending well. Pour into prepared pan; cool. With buttered scissors cut into 1-inch squares. Wrap individually.

About 6 dozen candies

Chocolate Surprise Truffles

Chocolate Surprise Truffles

- 1/2 cup unsalted butter, softened
- 2 1/2 cups confectioners' sugar
- 1/2 cup HERSHEY'S Cocoa
- 1/4 cup whipping cream
- 1 1/2 teaspoons vanilla extract
- Centers: Pecan or walnut halves, whole almonds, candied cherries, after-dinner mints
- Coatings: Confectioners' sugar, flaked coconut, chopped nuts

In large mixer bowl cream butter. Combine confectioners' sugar and cocoa; add alternately with whipping cream and vanilla to butter. Blend well. Chill until firm. Shape small amount of mixture around desired center; roll into 1-inch balls. Drop into desired coating and turn until well covered. Chill until firm.

About 3 dozen truffles

Chocolate Cream Filled Choco Tacos

- 8 taco shells
- 1 1/4 cups HERSHEY'S Semi-Sweet Chocolate Chips
- 1/3 cup butter or margarine
- 1 tablespoon milk
- 1 cup finely chopped pecans or walnuts
- Chocolate Cream Filling (recipe follows)
- 8 maraschino cherries (optional)

Heat oven to 350°. Place shells on cookie sheet. Heat 6 minutes; remove from oven. In shallow skillet over very low heat melt chocolate chips and butter, stirring constantly until chips are melted and mixture is smooth. Remove from heat. Stir in milk. Place nuts on wax paper-covered tray. Working with one shell at a time, dip entire outer surface in chocolate. Immediately coat outside of shell with nuts. Place coated shells on wax paper-covered cookie sheet to cool. Drizzle any remaining chocolate inside shells. Chill 1 to 2 hours or until chocolate hardens. About 2 hours before serving, prepare Chocolate Cream Filling. To serve, fill each shell with about 1/4 cup chilled filling. Garnish with reserved whipped cream mixture (from Chocolate Cream Filling) and maraschino cherry, if desired.

8 servings

Chocolate Cream Filling

- 3/4 cup HERSHEY'S Semi-Sweet Chocolate Chips
- 1/4 cup milk
- 1/2 teaspoon rum extract
- 1/2 teaspoon vanilla extract
- 2/3 cup marshmallow creme
- 1 cup chilled whipping cream
- 2 tablespoons confectioners' sugar

In small saucepan combine chocolate chips and milk; cook over low heat, stirring constantly, until chips are melted and mixture is smooth. Remove from heat. Stir in rum extract and vanilla. Pour mixture into large bowl; add marshmallow creme. Whisk until thoroughly blended. Cool. In small chilled mixer bowl beat whipping cream and confectioners' sugar until stiff. Reserve and refrigerate 1/2 cup whipped cream mixture for garnish. Gently fold remaining whipped cream mixture into chocolate mixture. Cover; freeze 1 to 1 1/2 hours to allow flavors to blend.

Recipe courtesy Mrs. Debbie Yandric, Hershey's THE GREAT AMERICAN CHOCOLATE FESTIVAL® program prize winner, and the Hershey Kitchens.

Chocolate Cream Filled Choco Taco

Chocolate Dipped Fruit

1 cup HERSHEY'S Semi-Sweet Chocolate Chips
1 tablespoon shortening (not butter, margarine or oil)
Assorted fresh fruit, washed and chilled

In top of double boiler over hot, not boiling, water melt chocolate chips and shortening; stir until smooth. Allow mixture to cool slightly. Dip fruit or fruit slices about 2/3 of the way into chocolate mixture. Shake gently to remove excess chocolate. Place on wax paper-covered tray. Chill, uncovered, about 30 minutes or until chocolate is firm.

About 1/2 cup coating

Microwave Directions: In small microwave-safe bowl melt chocolate chips and shortening at HIGH (100%) 1 to 1 1/2 minutes or just until chips are melted and mixture is smooth when stirred. Cool slightly. Dip and serve fruit as directed above.

Chocolate Petits Fours

4 eggs, separated
3/4 cup sugar, divided
3/4 cup ground blanched almonds
1/3 cup all-purpose flour
1/3 cup HERSHEY'S Cocoa
1/2 teaspoon baking soda
1/4 teaspoon salt
1/4 cup water
1 teaspoon vanilla extract
1/4 teaspoon almond extract
Semi-Sweet Chocolate Glaze (recipe follows)
Assorted decorating icing or gel

Heat oven to 375°. Line $15^1/_2 \times 10^1/_2 \times 1$-inch jelly roll pan with aluminum foil; generously grease foil. In small mixer bowl beat egg yolks on medium speed 3 minutes. Gradually add 1/2 cup sugar; continue beating 2 minutes. Combine almonds, flour, cocoa, baking soda and salt; add alternately with water to egg yolk mixture, beating just until blended. Stir in vanilla and almond extract. In large mixer bowl beat egg whites until foamy; gradually add remaining 1/4 cup sugar, beating until stiff peaks form. Carefully fold chocolate mixture into egg whites. Spread batter evenly in prepared pan. Bake 16 to 18 minutes or until top springs back when touched lightly. Carefully invert onto towel on wire rack; remove foil. Cool completely.

To prepare Petits Fours: With small cookie cutters (approximately 1 1/2-inch shapes) cut cake into assorted shapes. Place on wire rack with wax paper-covered cookie sheet under rack to catch drips when glazing. Spoon Semi-Sweet Chocolate Glaze over cake pieces until entire piece is covered. (Glaze that drips off can be reheated and used again.) Chill until glaze is set. Pipe decorations with icing or gel. Cover; store in cool place.

About 2 dozen petits fours

Semi-Sweet Chocolate Glaze

1 cup HERSHEY'S Semi-Sweet Chocolate Chips
1/4 cup unsalted butter
2 teaspoons vegetable oil

In top of double boiler over hot, not boiling, water melt chocolate chips with butter and oil, stirring until smooth. Cool slightly, stirring occasionally.

Microwave S'Mores

4 graham crackers
1 bar (1.65 ounces) HERSHEY'S Milk Chocolate Bar
4 large marshmallows

Break graham crackers in half. Break chocolate bar into 4 sections. Center one section on each of 4 graham cracker halves. Top each with marshmallow. Place on paper towel. Microwave at HIGH (100%) 10 to 15 seconds or until marshmallow puffs. Top each with another graham cracker half; press gently. Let stand 1 minute to soften chocolate. Serve immediately. *4 snacks*

VARIATION

Peanutty S'Mores: Spread thin layer of peanut butter on graham cracker or substitute 1.75-ounce bar MR. GOODBAR Chocolate Bar for milk chocolate bar. Proceed as directed.

Creamy Cocoa Taffy

Chocolate Mint Patties

3 2/3 cups (1 pound) confectioners' sugar
1/4 cup HERSHEY'S Cocoa
1/3 cup butter or margarine
1/3 cup light corn syrup
1 teaspoon peppermint extract
Decorator Frosting (recipe page 171)

Sift together confectioners' sugar and cocoa; set aside. In large mixer bowl on medium speed beat butter, corn syrup and peppermint extract until well blended. Gradually beat in 1 to 2 cups cocoa mixture until well blended and smooth. With wooden spoon stir in remaining cocoa mixture. With hands knead until mixture is well blended and smooth. On wax paper pat or roll out to 1/4-inch thickness. With small cookie cutters cut into desired shapes. Decorate using Decorator Frosting. Store in tightly covered container in refrigerator.

About 7 dozen mint patties

Chocolate Mint Patties

Creamy Cocoa Taffy

$1\frac{1}{4}$ cups sugar
$\frac{3}{4}$ cup light corn syrup
$\frac{1}{3}$ cup HERSHEY'S Cocoa
$\frac{1}{8}$ teaspoon salt
2 teaspoons white vinegar
$\frac{1}{4}$ cup evaporated milk
1 tablespoon butter

Butter 9-inch square pan; set aside. In heavy 2-quart saucepan combine sugar, corn syrup, cocoa, salt and vinegar. Cook over medium heat, stirring constantly, until mixture boils; add evaporated milk and butter. Continue cooking, stirring occasionally, to 248°F (firm-ball stage) on a candy thermometer or until syrup, when dropped into very cold water, forms a firm ball that does not flatten when removed from water. Pour mixture into prepared pan. Cool until lukewarm and comfortable to handle. Butter hands; immediately stretch taffy, folding and pulling until light in color and hard to pull. Place taffy on table; pull into $\frac{1}{2}$-inch-wide strips (twist two strips together, if desired). Cut into 1-inch pieces with buttered scissors. Wrap individually.

About $1\frac{1}{4}$ pounds candy

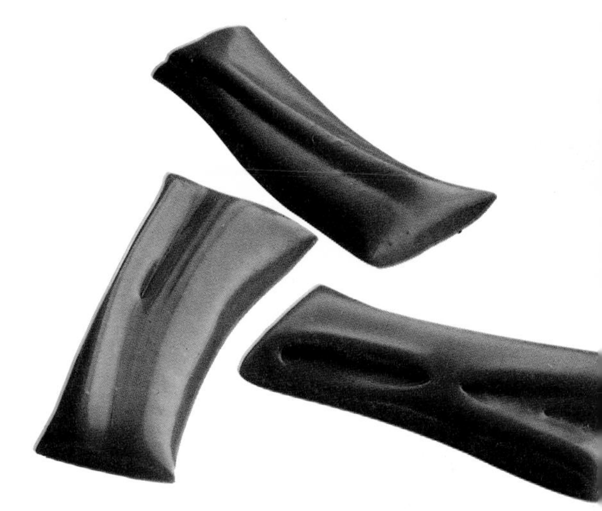

Peanutty-Cocoa Bonbons

- 2 packages (3 ounces each) cream cheese, softened
- 1 tablespoon milk
- 4 cups confectioners' sugar
- 1/3 cup HERSHEY'S Cocoa
- 1 teaspoon vanilla extract
- 1 cup finely chopped nuts (optional)
- Peanut Butter Coating (recipe follows)

In large mixer bowl beat cream cheese and milk until fluffy. Add confectioners' sugar, cocoa and vanilla; blend well. Stir in nuts, if desired. Cover; chill several hours or until firm enough to handle. To form centers shape into 1-inch balls. Place on wax paper-covered tray. Refrigerate, uncovered, 3 to 4 hours or until dry. Using long fork, dip cold centers into Peanut Butter coating. (To remove excess coating, slide fork across rim of pan and tap a few times.) Place on wax paper-covered tray; swirl coating on top of bonbon. If coating becomes too thick, reheat over hot water. OR reheat in microwave at HIGH (100%) 30 seconds. Refrigerate, uncovered, 1 hour. Store in airtight container in refrigerator.

About 10 dozen bonbons

Peanut Butter Coating

In top of double boiler over hot, not boiling, water melt 4 cups (two 12-ounce packages) REESE'S Peanut Butter Chips and 1/4 cup shortening (not butter, margarine or oil), stirring constantly to blend. Set aside; cool slightly.

Microwave Directions: Make centers as directed. In 1-quart microwave-safe bowl place peanut butter chips and shortening. Microwave at HIGH (100%) 1 to 2 minutes, stirring once, or just until chips are melted and mixture is smooth when stirred. Coat and store bonbons as directed.

Chocolate Truffles

3/4 cup butter
3/4 cup HERSHEY'S Cocoa
1 can (14 ounces) sweetened condensed milk
1 tablespoon vanilla extract
Cocoa or confectioners' sugar

In heavy saucepan over low heat melt butter. Add cocoa; stir until smooth. Blend in sweetened condensed milk; stir constantly until mixture is thick, smooth and glossy, about 4 minutes. Remove from heat; stir in vanilla. Chill 3 to 4 hours or until firm. Shape into 1 1/4-inch balls; roll in cocoa or confectioners' sugar. Chill until firm, 1 to 2 hours. Store, covered, in refrigerator.

About 2 1/2 dozen candies

VARIATIONS

Nut Truffles: Add 3/4 cup coarsely chopped toasted pecans to chocolate mixture when adding vanilla. (To toast pecans: Toast 3/4 cup pecan halves in shallow baking pan in 350° oven, stirring occasionally, 6 to 8 minutes or until golden brown. Cool.)

Rum Nut Truffles: Decrease vanilla to 1 teaspoon. Stir in 2 to 3 tablespoons rum or 1 teaspoon rum extract and 3/4 cup coarsely chopped toasted nuts.

Espresso Truffles: Decrease vanilla to 1 teaspoon. Stir in 1 1/4 teaspoons instant espresso coffee with vanilla. Roll balls in cocoa or chopped nuts.

Nut-Coated Truffles: Roll balls in chopped nuts.

Rich Cocoa Fudge

3 cups sugar
$^2/_3$ cup HERSHEY'S Cocoa
$^1/_8$ teaspoon salt
1$^1/_2$ cups milk
$^1/_4$ cup butter or margarine
1 teaspoon vanilla extract
Pecan halves (optional)

Butter 8- or 9-inch square pan; set aside. In heavy 4-quart saucepan combine sugar, cocoa and salt; stir in milk. Cook over medium heat, stirring constantly, until mixture comes to full rolling boil. Boil, without stirring, to 234°F on a candy thermometer (soft-ball stage) or until syrup, when dropped into very cold water, forms soft ball that flattens when removed from water. (Bulb of candy thermometer should *not* rest on bottom of saucepan.) Remove from heat. Add butter and vanilla. *Do not stir.* Cool at room temperature to 110°F (lukewarm). Beat until fudge thickens and loses some of its gloss. Quickly spread into prepared pan. Cool. Cut into squares. Garnish with pecan halves, if desired.

About 3 dozen candies

VARIATIONS

Nutty Rich Cocoa Fudge: Beat cooked fudge as directed. Immediately stir in 1 cup broken almonds, pecans or walnuts and quickly spread into prepared pan.

Marshmallow-Nut Cocoa Fudge: Increase cocoa to $^3/_4$ cup; cook fudge as directed above. Add 1 cup marshmallow creme with butter and vanilla. *Do not stir.* Cool to 110°F (lukewarm). Beat 10 minutes; stir in 1 cup broken nuts and pour into prepared pan. (Fudge does not set until poured into pan.)

Chocolate Orange Balls

1 package (12 ounces) vanilla wafer cookies
3/4 cup confectioners' sugar
1 1/2 cups chopped nuts
1/4 cup HERSHEY'S Cocoa
3 tablespoons light corn syrup
1/2 cup orange juice
1 teaspoon grated orange peel
Additional confectioners' sugar

Finely crush vanilla wafer cookies. In large bowl combine crushed wafers, 3/4 cup confectioners' sugar, nuts and cocoa. Blend in corn syrup, orange juice and peel. Shape into 1-inch balls; roll in confectioners' sugar. Store in airtight container 2 to 3 days to develop flavor. Reroll before serving. *About 4 dozen balls*

HOW TO COAT CANDY

You can make professional-looking candies by using HERSHEY'S "Simple Chocolate Coating." Neither wax nor special confectioners' coating is needed with this method.

Making the Centers
Select the recipes for the center you wish to coat and prepare them at least a day ahead. For variety, try different shapes.

Choosing the Right Day
Don't try to make and use coating on a humid day! Humidity, steam or wet equipment cause chocolate to thicken, tighten and become grainy. Even a few drops of water can cause problems. Make sure all utensils are dry before beginning and no water gets into the chocolate mixture while melting.

Assembling the Equipment
Before you begin the coating process, assemble the equipment you need:

- Tape, wax paper and tray.
- A thermometer that registers as low as 80°F is useful, but not necessary (most ordinary candy thermometers do not register below 100°F).
- Rubber scraper.
- Glass bowl or glass measuring cup to hold the chocolate and shortening.
- Larger glass bowl or a pan to hold the warm water.
- Fondue fork or table fork to dip the centers into coating.

If the instructions are followed *exactly*, glossy chocolate-coated centers will stay firm at room temperature, without "bloom". (Bloom is white or gray spots or streaks that appear when sugar or fat particles separate from chocolate).

The success of this method depends on the very slow melting and constant stirring of the chocolate. With patience and a little practice, you can enjoy professional results.

Helpful Hints

1. Constant scraping and stirring, as stated in the instructions, will help insure success; they are necessary for proper crystal formation.
2. Use solid vegetable shortening as directed, NOT butter, margarine or oil. Butter and margarine contain moisture that can cause chocolate to tighten and become grainy.

Easy Buttercream Centers

1 package (3 ounces) cream cheese, softened
1/2 cup butter, softened
4 cups confectioners' sugar
1 1/2 teaspoons vanilla extract

1. In large mixer bowl beat cream cheese and butter until smooth.
2. Blend in confectioners' sugar and vanilla. (If necessary, chill about 1 hour or until mixture is firm enough to handle.)
3. Shape into 1-inch balls; place on wax paper-covered tray.
4. Cover loosely; chill 3 to 4 hours or overnight. Centers should feel dry to the touch before coating.
5. Coat centers as directed.

About 5 dozen centers

VARIATIONS

Chocolate Buttercream Centers: Blend 1/3 cup HERSHEY'S Cocoa with confectioners' sugar and vanilla extract into above mixture. Add 1 to 2 teaspoons milk until mixture holds together.

Flavored Buttercream Centers

Divide buttercream mixture into three parts. Add any of the following to each part:

2/3 cup flaked coconut
1/2 teaspoon brandy extract or almond extract
1/2 teaspoon strawberry extract plus 3 drops red food color
1/4 teaspoon rum extract or orange extract
1/4 teaspoon mint extract plus 3 drops green food color

Prepare an assortment of centers in advance. Chill until ready to coat with chocolate.

Combine chocolate and shortening in completely dry bowl. Don't let even one drop of water into mixture!

Chocolate-shortening mixture must be stirred and scraped down "constantly" with rubber spatula.

Chocolate mixture should be completely fluid and very smooth before starting to coat centers.

When coating is ready, rest a center on fork; carefully and completely dip into chocolate mixture. Tap fork on side of bowl to remove excess coating.

Invert center onto prepared cookie sheet. Using tip of fork, decorate top of candy with small amount of melted chocolate.

Simple Chocolate Coating

2 cups (12-ounce package) HERSHEY'S Semi-Sweet Chocolate Chips or MINI CHIPS Chocolate
2 tablespoons plus 2 teaspoons shortening (NOT butter, margarine or oil)

1. Place chocolate and shortening in 1-quart heatproof glass measuring cup or 1½ quart heatproof glass bowl. Fill another larger heatproof glass bowl or large pan with 1 inch of very warm tap water (100°-110°F).
2. Place measuring cup or bowl containing chocolate in the larger bowl or pan so that water covers bottom half of cup or bowl containing chocolate. (Keep water level low so that water does not get into the chocolate mixture and ruin the coating.)
3. Stir CONSTANTLY with rubber scraper until chocolate is completely melted and mixture is smooth. DO NOT RUSH. It will take at least 20 minutes to melt chocolate.
4. If water cools, pour it out and add more warm water (100°-110°F). (Be careful not to get any water into the chocolate mixture.) Remove the measuring cup or bowl containing the melted chocolate mixture from water. Chocolate mixture should be between 84° and 88°F.
5. Dip chilled centers completely into chocolate mixture, one at a time, with fork.
6. Gently tap fork on side of cup or bowl to remove excess chocolate. Invert coated center onto wax paper-covered tray; decorate top of coated center with small amount of melted chocolate, using tip of fork.
7. Store coated centers, loosely covered, in a cool, dry place.

Coats about 5 dozen centers

COOKIES & COOKIE BARS

Here's all kinds of cookies to choose from—all made delicious with chocolate.

Five Layer Bars (left) and Cocoa Cherry Drops (recipes page 144)

Cocoa Cherry Drops

- 1/2 cup plus 2 tablespoons butter or margarine
- 1 cup sugar
- 1 egg
- 1 teaspoon vanilla extract
- 1 1/4 cups all-purpose flour
- 6 tablespoons HERSHEY'S Cocoa
- 1/2 teaspoon baking soda
- 1/2 teaspoon salt
- 1 cup chopped maraschino cherries, well drained
- 1/2 cup chopped walnuts
- Walnut pieces (optional)

Heat oven to 350°. In large mixer bowl cream butter and sugar. Beat in egg and vanilla. Combine flour, cocoa, baking soda and salt; blend into creamed mixture. Stir in cherries and chopped walnuts. Drop by rounded teaspoonfuls onto ungreased cookie sheet. Press walnut piece into each cookie, if desired. Bake 10 to 12 minutes or until set. Cool slightly; remove from cookie sheet to wire rack. Cool completely.

About 4 dozen cookies

Five Layer Bars

- 3/4 cup butter or margarine
- 1 3/4 cups graham cracker crumbs
- 1/4 cup HERSHEY'S Cocoa
- 2 tablespoons sugar
- 1 can (14 ounces) sweetened condensed milk
- 1 cup HERSHEY'S Semi-Sweet Chocolate Chips
- 1 cup raisins or chopped dried apricots or miniature marshmallows
- 1 cup chopped nuts

Heat oven to 350°. In 13 x 9 x 2-inch baking pan melt butter in oven. Combine crumbs, cocoa and sugar; sprinkle over butter. Pour sweetened condensed milk evenly over crumbs. Sprinkle chocolate chips and raisins over sweetened condensed milk. Sprinkle nuts on top; press down firmly. Bake 25 to 30 minutes or until lightly browned. Cool completely; cover with aluminum foil. Let stand at room temperature about 8 hours before cutting into bars.

About 3 dozen bars

VARIATION

Golden Bars: Substitute 1 cup REESE'S Peanut Butter Chips for chocolate chips. Sprinkle 1 cup golden raisins or chopped dried apricots over chips. Proceed as above.

Chewy Chocolate Macaroons

- 1 package (14 ounces) flaked coconut (about 5 1/3 cups)
- 1/2 cup HERSHEY'S Cocoa
- 1 can (14 ounces) sweetened condensed milk
- 2 teaspoons vanilla extract
- Red candied cherries, halved

Heat oven to 350°. In large bowl thoroughly combine coconut and cocoa; stir in sweetened condensed milk and vanilla. Drop by rounded teaspoonfuls onto generously greased cookie sheet. Press cherry half into each cookie. Bake 8 to 10 minutes or until almost set. Immediately remove from cookie sheet to wire rack. Cool completely. Store loosely covered at room temperature.

About 4 dozen cookies

Buried Cherry Cookies

- Chocolate Frosting (recipe follows)
- 1/2 cup butter or margarine
- 1 cup sugar
- 1 egg
- 1 1/2 teaspoons vanilla extract
- 1 1/2 cups all-purpose flour
- 1/3 cup HERSHEY'S Cocoa
- 1/4 teaspoon baking powder
- 1/4 teaspoon baking soda
- 1/4 teaspoon salt
- 1 jar (10 ounces) small maraschino cherries (about 44)

Prepare Chocolate Frosting; set aside. Heat oven to 350°. In large mixer bowl cream butter, sugar, egg and vanilla until light and fluffy. Combine flour, cocoa, baking powder, baking soda and salt; gradually add to creamed mixture until well blended. Shape dough into 1-inch balls. Place about 2 inches apart on ungreased cookie sheet. Press thumb gently in center of each cookie. Drain cherries; place one cherry in center of each cookie. Bake 10 minutes or until edges are set; remove from cookie sheet to wire rack. Spoon scant teaspoonful frosting over cherry, spreading to cover cherry.

About 3 1/2 dozen cookies

Chocolate Frosting

- 2/3 cup sweetened condensed milk
- 1/2 cup HERSHEY'S Semi-Sweet Chocolate Chips

In small saucepan combine sweetened condensed milk and chocolate chips. Stir constantly over low heat until chips are melted and mixture is smooth, about 5 minutes. Remove from heat; cool thoroughly.

Marbled Brownies

- Nut Cream Filling (recipe follows)
- 1/2 cup butter or margarine
- 1/3 cup HERSHEY'S Cocoa
- 2 eggs
- 1 cup sugar
- 1 teaspoon vanilla extract
- 1/2 cup all-purpose flour
- 1/2 teaspoon baking powder
- 1/4 teaspoon salt

Prepare Nut Cream Filling; set aside. Heat oven to 350°. Grease 9-inch square baking pan. In small saucepan melt butter; remove from heat. Blend in cocoa; set aside to cool slightly. In small mixer bowl beat eggs until foamy. Gradually add sugar and vanilla; blend well. Combine flour, baking powder and salt; blend into egg mixture. Stir in chocolate mixture. Remove 3/4 cup batter; set aside. Spread remaining batter into prepared pan. Spread Nut Cream Filling over chocolate. Drop teaspoonfuls of reserved chocolate over top. Swirl gently with metal spatula or knife to marble. Bake 35 to 40 minutes or until brownies begin to pull away from sides of pan. Cool completely. Cut into squares. *About 20 brownies*

Nut Cream Filling

1 package (3 ounces) cream cheese, softened
2 tablespoons butter or margarine, softened
1/4 cup sugar
1 egg
1/2 teaspoon vanilla extract
1/4 to 1/2 teaspoon almond extract
1 tablespoon all-purpose flour
1/4 cup slivered almonds, toasted and chopped*

In small mixer bowl beat cream cheese, butter and sugar until creamy. Blend in egg, vanilla and almond extract. Stir in flour and almonds.

*To toast almonds: Toast in shallow baking pan in 350° oven, stirring occasionally, 8 to 10 minutes or until golden brown. Cool.

Honey Brownies

1/3 cup butter or margarine
1/2 cup sugar
1/3 cup honey
2 teaspoons vanilla extract
2 eggs
1/2 cup all-purpose flour
1/3 cup HERSHEY'S Cocoa
1/2 teaspoon salt
2/3 cup chopped nuts
Creamy Brownie Frosting (optional, recipe page 156)

Heat oven to 350°. Grease 9-inch square baking pan. In small mixer bowl cream butter and sugar; blend in honey and vanilla. Add eggs; beat well. Combine flour, cocoa and salt; gradually add to creamed mixture. Stir in nuts. Spread into prepared pan. Bake 25 to 30 minutes or until brownies begin to pull away from sides of pan. Cool completely. Frost with Creamy Brownie Frosting, if desired. Cut into squares.

About 16 brownies

Chocolate Chip 'n Oatmeal Cookies

- 1 package (18.25 or 18.5 ounces) yellow cake mix
- 1 cup quick-cooking rolled oats
- 3/4 cup butter or margarine, softened
- 2 eggs
- 1 cup HERSHEY'S Semi-Sweet Chocolate Chips

Heat oven to 350°. In large mixer bowl combine cake mix, oats, butter and eggs; mix well. Stir in chocolate chips. Drop by rounded teaspoonfuls onto ungreased cookie sheet. Bake 10 to 12 minutes or until very lightly browned. Cool slightly; remove from cookie sheet to wire rack. Cool completely.

About 4 dozen cookies

Easy Peanutty Snickerdoodles

- 2 tablespoons sugar
- 2 teaspoons ground cinnamon
- 1 package (15 ounces) golden sugar cookie mix
- 1 egg
- 1 tablespoon water
- 1 cup REESE'S Peanut Butter Chips

Heat oven to 375°. In small bowl combine sugar and cinnamon. In medium bowl combine cookie mix (and enclosed flavor packet), egg and water; mix with spoon or fork until thoroughly blended. Stir in peanut butter chips. Shape dough into 1-inch balls. (If dough is too soft, cover and chill about 1 hour.) Roll balls in cinnamon-sugar. Place on ungreased cookie sheet. Bake 8 to 10 minutes or until very lightly browned. Cool slightly; remove from cookie sheet to wire rack. Cool completely.

About 2 dozen cookies

Chocolate Kiss Cookies

- 1 package (15 ounces) golden sugar cookie mix
- 1/2 cup HERSHEY'S Cocoa
- 1 egg
- 2 tablespoons water
- 3/4 cup finely chopped nuts
- 1 bag (9 ounces) HERSHEY'S KISSES Chocolates, unwrapped (about 42)

Heat oven to 350°. In medium bowl combine cookie mix (and enclosed flavor packet), cocoa, egg and water; mix with spoon or fork until thoroughly blended. Shape dough into 1-inch balls. Roll balls in nuts; place on ungreased cookie sheet. Bake 8 minutes. Immediately press KISS into center of each warm cookie, allowing cookie to crack slightly. Cool slightly; remove from cookie sheet to wire rack. Cool completely.

About 3 1/2 dozen cookies

From top to bottom: Chocolate Chip 'n Oatmeal Cookies, Easy Peanutty Snickerdoodles and Chocolate Kiss Cookies

English Toffee Bars

English Toffee Bars

2 cups all-purpose flour
1 cup packed light brown sugar
1/2 cup butter
1 cup pecan halves
Toffee Topping (recipe follows)
1 cup HERSHEY'S Milk Chocolate Chips

Heat oven to 350°. In large mixer bowl combine flour, brown sugar and butter; mix until fine crumbs form. (A few large crumbs may remain.) Press into ungreased 13×9×2-inch baking pan. Sprinkle pecans over crust. Drizzle Toffee Topping evenly over pecans and crust. Bake 20 to 22 minutes or until topping is bubbly and golden. Remove from oven. Immediately sprinkle chocolate chips over top; press gently onto surface. Cool completely. Cut into bars.

About 3 dozen bars

Toffee Topping

In small saucepan combine 2/3 cup butter and 1/3 cup packed light brown sugar. Cook over medium heat, stirring constantly, until mixture comes to boil; boil and stir 30 seconds. Use immediately.

Butter Pecan Squares

1/2 cup butter, softened
1/2 cup packed light brown sugar
1 egg
1 teaspoon vanilla extract
3/4 cup all-purpose flour
2 cups HERSHEY'S Milk Chocolate Chips, divided
3/4 cup chopped pecans, divided

Heat oven to 350°. Grease 8- or 9-inch square baking pan. In small mixer bowl cream butter, sugar, egg and vanilla until light and fluffy. Blend in flour. Stir in 1 cup milk chocolate chips and 1/2 cup pecans. Spread into prepared pan. Bake 25 to 30 minutes or until lightly browned. Remove from oven. Immediately sprinkle remaining 1 cup chips over surface. Let stand 5 to 10 minutes or until chips soften; spread evenly. Immediately sprinkle remaining 1/4 cup pecans over top; press gently onto chocolate. Cool completely. Cut into squares.

About 16 squares

Butter Pecan Squares

Drizzle Topped Brownies

Drizzle Topped Brownies

1 1/4 cups all-purpose biscuit baking mix
1 cup sugar
1/2 cup HERSHEY'S Cocoa
1/2 cup butter or margarine, melted
2 eggs
1 teaspoon vanilla extract
1 cup HERSHEY'S Semi-Sweet Chocolate Chips or MINI CHIPS
Quick Vanilla Glaze (recipe follows)

Heat oven to 350°. Grease 8- or 9-inch square baking pan. In medium bowl combine baking mix, sugar and cocoa; mix with spoon or fork until thoroughly blended. Add butter, eggs and vanilla, mixing well. Stir in chocolate chips. Spread into prepared pan. Bake 25 to 30 minutes or until wooden pick inserted in center comes out clean. Cool completely. Drizzle Quick Vanilla Glaze over cooled brownies. Cut into bars. *About 20 brownies*

Quick Vanilla Glaze

In small bowl combine 1/2 cup confectioners' sugar, 1 tablespoon water and 1/4 teaspoon vanilla extract; blend well.

Cocoa Crispy Treats

6 tablespoons butter or margarine
1/4 cup peanut butter
1 package (10 ounces) regular marshmallows (about 40) or 4 cups miniature marshmallows
1/3 cup HERSHEY'S Cocoa
4 cups crisped rice cereal
1/2 cup unsalted peanuts or REESE'S Peanut Butter Chips or HERSHEY'S Semi-Sweet Chocolate Chips

Butter 9-inch square pan. In large saucepan over low heat melt butter and peanut butter. Add marshmallows and stir until completely melted and well blended. Remove from heat. Stir in cocoa; blend well. Add cereal and peanuts. Stir until cereal is well coated. Using buttered spatula or wax paper, press mixture evenly into prepared pan. Cool completely. Cut into squares. *About 16 squares*

Chocolate Teddy Bears

2/3 cup butter or margarine
1 cup sugar
2 teaspoons vanilla extract
2 eggs
2 1/2 cups all-purpose flour
1/2 cup HERSHEY'S Cocoa
1/2 teaspoon baking soda
1/4 teaspoon salt

In large mixer bowl cream butter, sugar and vanilla until light and fluffy. Add eggs; blend well. Combine flour, cocoa, baking soda and salt; gradually add to creamed mixture, blending thoroughly. Chill until dough is firm enough to handle. Heat oven to 350°.

To shape teddy bears: For each cookie, form a portion of the dough into 1 large ball for body (1 to 1 1/2 inches), 1 medium-size ball for head (3/4 to 1 inch), 4 small balls for arms and legs (1/2 inch), 2 smaller balls for ears, 1 tiny ball for nose and 4 tiny balls for paws (optional). On ungreased cookie sheet flatten large ball slightly for body. Attach medium-size ball for head by overlapping slightly onto body. Place balls for arms, legs and ears, and a tiny ball on head for nose. Arrange other tiny balls atop ends of legs and arms for paws, if desired. With wooden pick, draw eyes and mouth; pierce small hole at top of cookie for use as hanging ornament, if desired. Bake 6 to 8 minutes or until set. Cool 1 minute; remove from cookie sheet to wire rack. Cool completely. Store in covered container. If cookies will be used as ornaments, allow to dry on wire rack at least 6 hours before hanging. Decorate with ribbon or pull ribbon through hole for hanging, if desired. *About 14 cookies*

Chocolate-Filled Walnut-Oatmeal Bars

- 1 cup butter or margarine, softened
- 2 cups packed light brown sugar
- 2 eggs
- 1 teaspoon vanilla extract
- 1/2 teaspoon powdered instant coffee (optional)
- 3 cups quick-cooking rolled oats
- 2 1/2 cups all-purpose flour
- 1 teaspoon baking soda
- 1/2 teaspoon salt
- 1 1/2 cups chopped walnuts, divided
- Chocolate Filling (recipe follows)

Heat oven to 350°. In large mixer bowl cream butter and brown sugar until light and fluffy. Add eggs, vanilla and instant coffee, if desired; beat well. Combine oats, flour, baking soda, salt and 1 cup walnuts; gradually add to creamed mixture. (Batter will be stiff; stir in last part by hand.) Remove 2 cups dough; set aside. Press remaining dough evenly onto bottom of 15 1/2 × 10 1/2 × 1-inch jelly-roll pan. Spread Chocolate Filling evenly over oatmeal mixture in pan. Sprinkle remaining oatmeal mixture over chocolate. Sprinkle remaining 1/2 cup walnuts over top. Bake 25 minutes or until top is golden (chocolate will be soft). Cool completely. Cut into bars.

About 4 dozen bars

Chocolate Filling

- 1/2 cup butter or margarine
- 2/3 cup HERSHEY'S Cocoa
- 1/4 cup sugar
- 1 can (14 ounces) sweetened condensed milk
- 1 1/2 teaspoons vanilla extract

In medium saucepan over low heat melt butter. Stir in cocoa and sugar. Add sweetened condensed milk; cook, stirring constantly, until smooth and thick. Remove from heat. Stir in vanilla.

Chocolate Cookie Pretzels

- 2/3 cup butter or margarine
- 1 cup granulated sugar
- 2 teaspoons vanilla extract
- 2 eggs
- 2 1/2 cups all-purpose flour
- 1/2 cup HERSHEY'S Cocoa
- 1/2 teaspoon baking soda
- 1/4 teaspoon salt
- Confectioners' sugar or Satiny Chocolate Glaze (recipe page 159) or Peanut Butter Chip Frosting (optional, recipe follows)

Heat oven to 350°. In large mixer bowl cream butter, granulated sugar and vanilla until light and fluffy. Add eggs; blend well. Combine flour, cocoa, baking soda and salt; gradually add to creamed mixture, blending thoroughly. Divide dough into 24 pieces. On lightly floured surface roll each piece with hands into pencil-like strip, about 12 inches long. Place strip on ungreased cookie sheet. Twist into pretzel shape by crossing left side of strip to middle, forming loop. Fold right side up and over first loop. Place about 2 inches apart on cookie sheet. Bake 8 minutes or until set. Cool 1 minute; remove from cookie sheet to wire rack. Cool completely. Sprinkle confectioners' sugar over cookies OR frost with Satiny Chocolate Glaze or Peanut Butter Chip Frosting, if desired.

2 dozen cookies

Peanut Butter Chip Frosting

- 1 cup confectioners' sugar
- 1/4 cup butter or margarine
- 3 tablespoons milk
- 1 cup REESE'S Peanut Butter Chips
- 1/2 teaspoon vanilla extract

Place confectioners' sugar in small mixer bowl; set aside. In small saucepan combine butter, milk and peanut butter chips. Cook over low heat, stirring constantly, until chips are melted and mixture is smooth. Remove from heat. Add warm mixture to confectioners' sugar; blend in vanilla. Beat until smooth. Spread while warm.

About 1 cup frosting

Giant Chocolate Oatmeal Cookies

- 1 cup shortening
- 1 3/4 cups packed light brown sugar
- 3 eggs
- 2 teaspoons vanilla extract
- 1 1/3 cups all-purpose flour
- 1/2 cup HERSHEY'S Cocoa
- 2 teaspoons baking soda
- 1/4 teaspoon salt
- 1/2 cup water
- 1 cup flaked coconut
- 1 cup raisins
- 1 cup REESE'S Peanut Butter Chips
- 3 cups quick-cooking rolled oats
- Additional REESE'S Peanut Butter Chips and coconut (optional)

In large mixer bowl beat shortening, brown sugar, eggs and vanilla until light and fluffy. Combine flour, cocoa, baking soda and salt; add alternately with water to shortening mixture. Add coconut, raisins, peanut butter chips and oats; blend well. Cover; chill 2 hours. Heat oven to 350°. Using a 1/4 cup ice cream scoop or measuring cup, drop dough about 4 inches apart onto lightly greased cookie sheet. Sprinkle additional chips and coconut on top, if desired. Bake 10 to 12 minutes or until set (do not overbake). Cool slightly; remove from cookie sheet to wire rack. Cool completely.

About 3 dozen 3-inch cookies

Form pretzel by crossing left side of strip to middle, forming loop.

Fold right side up and over loop to complete pretzel shape.

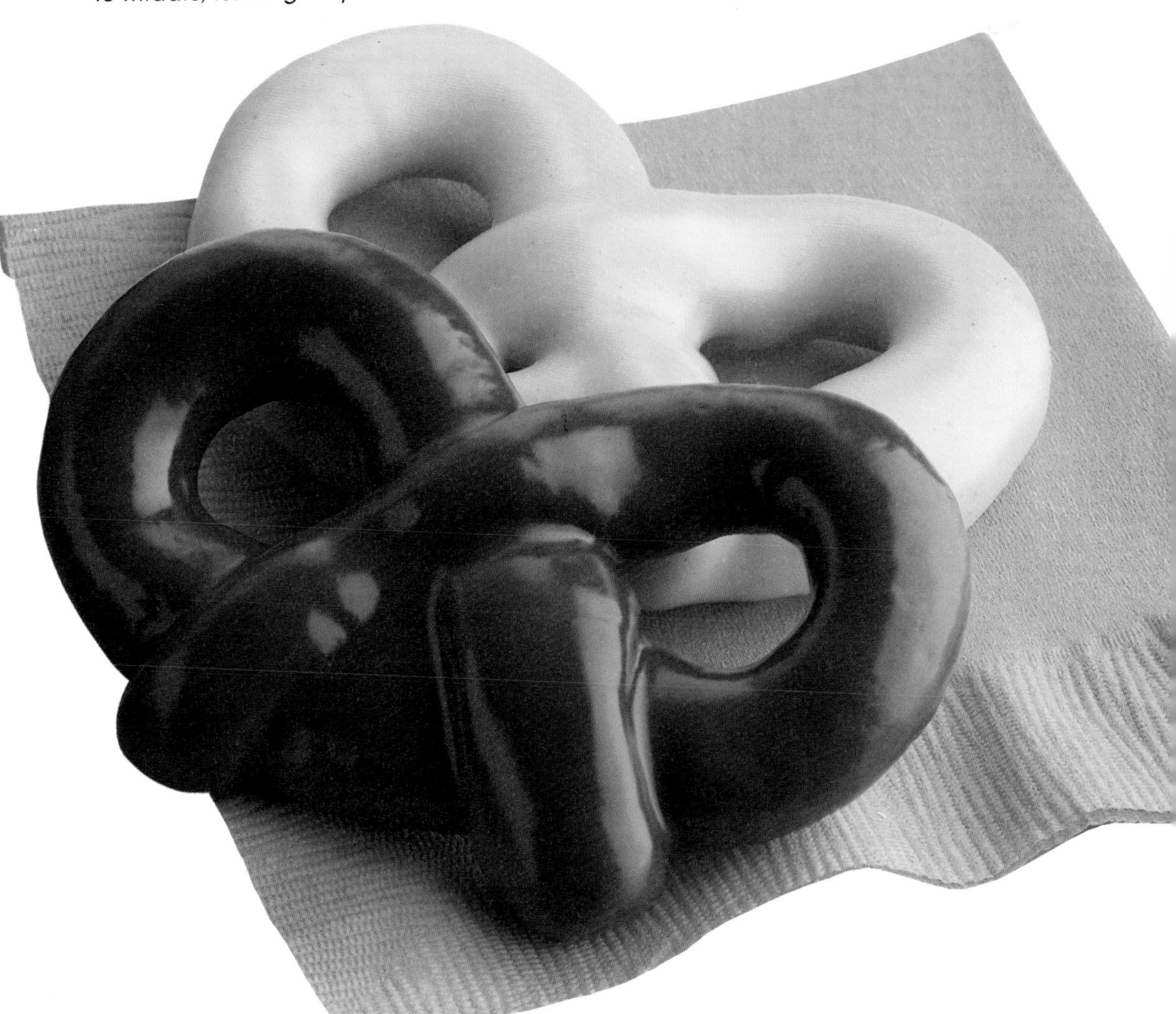

Best Brownies

Creamy Brownie Frosting

- 3 tablespoons butter or margarine, softened
- 3 tablespoons HERSHEY'S Cocoa
- 1 tablespoon light corn syrup or honey
- ½ teaspoon vanilla extract
- 1 cup confectioners' sugar
- 1 to 2 tablespoons milk

In small mixer bowl beat butter, cocoa, corn syrup and vanilla. Add confectioners' sugar and milk; beat to spreading consistency.

About 1 cup frosting

Best Brownies

- ½ cup butter or margarine, melted
- 1 cup sugar
- 1 teaspoon vanilla extract
- 2 eggs
- ½ cup all-purpose flour
- ⅓ cup HERSHEY'S Cocoa
- ¼ teaspoon baking powder
- ¼ teaspoon salt
- ½ cup chopped walnuts (optional)
- Creamy Brownie Frosting (optional, recipe follows)
- Walnut halves (optional)

Heat oven to 350°. Grease 9-inch square baking pan. In large bowl blend butter, sugar and vanilla. Add eggs; using spoon, beat well. Combine flour, cocoa, baking powder and salt; gradually add to egg mixture, beating until well blended. Stir in nuts, if desired. Spread into prepared pan. Bake 20 to 25 minutes or until brownies begin to pull away from sides of pan. Cool completely. Frost with Creamy Brownie Frosting, if desired. Cut into squares. Garnish with walnut halves, if desired.

About 16 brownies

Luscious Layered Bars

- ½ cup butter or margarine
- 1 package (18.25 or 18.5 ounces) chocolate cake mix
- 1 cup HERSHEY'S Semi-Sweet Chocolate Chips
- 1 cup REESE'S Peanut Butter Chips
- 1 cup shredded coconut
- 1 cup coarsely chopped walnuts or pecans
- 1 can (14 ounces) sweetened condensed milk

Heat oven to 325°. Grease 15½ × 10½ × 1-inch jelly-roll pan. Cut butter into cake mix with pastry blender or fork to form coarse crumbs; sprinkle evenly in prepared pan. Sprinkle chocolate chips, peanut butter chips, coconut and nuts over crumb mixture. Drizzle sweetened condensed milk evenly over top. Bake 30 to 35 minutes or until slightly bubbly and very lightly browned. Cool completely. Cut into bars.

About 4 dozen bars

Double Chocolate Black-Eyed Susans

- 1 package (18.25 or 19.75 ounces) fudge marble cake mix
- 1 egg
- 1/3 cup vegetable oil
- 4 tablespoons water, divided
- 1 cup HERSHEY'S MINI CHIPS Semi-Sweet Chocolate

Heat oven to 350°. In large bowl combine cake mix, egg, oil and 3 tablespoons water; mix with spoon until thoroughly blended. Stir in MINI CHIPS Chocolate. In small bowl combine 2/3 cup batter, chocolate packet from cake mix and remaining 1 tablespoon water; mix well. Drop vanilla batter by rounded teaspoonfuls onto lightly greased cookie sheet; press thumb or back of spoon gently in center of each cookie. Drop chocolate batter by rounded half-teaspoonfuls onto top of each cookie. Bake 10 to 12 minutes or until very lightly browned. Cool slightly; remove from cookie sheet to wire rack. Cool completely.

About 3 dozen cookies

No-Bake Cocoa Haystacks

1 1/2 cups sugar
1/2 cup butter or margarine
1/2 cup milk
1/2 cup HERSHEY'S Cocoa
1 teaspoon vanilla extract
3 1/2 cups quick-cooking rolled oats
1 cup flaked coconut
1/2 cup chopped nuts

In medium saucepan combine sugar, butter, milk and cocoa. Cook over medium heat, stirring constantly, until mixture comes to full boil; remove from heat. Stir in remaining ingredients. Immediately drop by rounded teaspoonfuls onto wax paper. Cool completely. Store in cool, dry place.

About 4 dozen cookies

Spiced Chip Cookies

1 package (18.25 or 18.5 ounces) spice cake mix
1 cup quick-cooking rolled oats
3/4 cup butter or margarine, softened
2 eggs
2 cups HERSHEY'S Milk Chocolate Chips
1/2 cup coarsely chopped nuts

Heat oven to 350°. In large mixer bowl combine cake mix, oats, butter and eggs; mix well. Stir in milk chocolate chips and nuts. Drop by rounded teaspoonfuls onto ungreased cookie sheet. Bake 10 to 12 minutes or until very lightly browned. Cool slightly; remove from cookie sheet to wire rack. Cool completely.

About 4 dozen cookies

Cut Out Chocolate Cookies

1/2 cup butter or margarine
3/4 cup sugar
1 egg
1 teaspoon vanilla extract
1 1/2 cups all-purpose flour
1/3 cup HERSHEY'S Cocoa
1/2 teaspoon baking powder
1/2 teaspoon baking soda
1/4 teaspoon salt
Satiny Chocolate Glaze or Vanilla Glaze (recipes follow)

In large mixer bowl cream butter, sugar, egg and vanilla until light and fluffy. Combine flour, cocoa, baking powder, baking soda and salt; add to creamed mixture, blending well. Chill dough about 1 hour or until firm enough to roll. Heat oven to 325°. On lightly floured board or between 2 pieces of wax paper, roll small portion of dough at a time to 1/4-inch thickness. Cut into desired shapes with cookie cutters; place on ungreased cookie sheet. Bake 5 to 7 minutes or until no indentation remains when touched lightly. Cool slightly; remove from cookie sheet to wire rack. Cool completely. Frost with Satiny Chocolate Glaze or Vanilla Glaze. Decorate as desired.

About 3 dozen cookies

Satiny Chocolate Glaze

2 tablespoons butter or margarine
3 tablespoons HERSHEY'S Cocoa
2 tablespoons water
½ teaspoon vanilla extract
1 cup confectioners' sugar

In small saucepan over low heat melt butter. Add cocoa and water. Cook, stirring constantly, until mixture thickens; *do not boil*. Remove from heat; add vanilla. Gradually add confectioners' sugar, beating with wire whisk until smooth. Add additional water, ½ teaspoon at a time, until desired consistency.

About ¾ cup glaze

Vanilla Glaze

3 tablespoons butter or margarine
2 cups confectioners' sugar
1 teaspoon vanilla extract
2 to 3 tablespoons milk
2 to 4 drops food color (optional)

In small saucepan over low heat melt butter. Remove from heat; blend in confectioners' sugar and vanilla. Gradually add milk, beating with spoon or wire whisk until desired consistency. Blend in food color, if desired.

About 1 cup glaze

Cut Out Chocolate Cookies

Chocolate-Cherry Squares

1 cup all-purpose flour
1/3 cup butter or margarine
1/2 cup packed light brown sugar
1/2 cup chopped nuts
Filling (recipe follows)
Red candied cherries, halved

Heat oven to 350°. In large mixer bowl combine flour, butter and brown sugar. Blend on low speed 2 to 3 minutes to form fine crumbs. Stir in nuts. Reserve 3/4 cup crumb mixture for topping; pat remaining crumbs into ungreased 9-inch square baking pan. Bake 10 minutes or until lightly browned. Meanwhile, prepare Filling; spread over warm crust. Sprinkle reserved crumb mixture over top; garnish with cherry halves. Return to oven; bake 25 minutes or until lightly browned. Cool. Cut into squares. Store, covered, in refrigerator.

About 3 dozen squares

Filling

1 package (8 ounces) cream cheese, softened
1/2 cup sugar
1/3 cup HERSHEY'S Cocoa
1/4 cup milk
1 egg
1/4 teaspoon vanilla extract
1/4 cup chopped red candied cherries

In small mixer bowl beat cream cheese and sugar until fluffy. Add cocoa, milk, egg and vanilla; beat until smooth. Fold in cherries.

Chocolate Crinkle Cookies

Chocolate Crinkle Cookies

- 2 cups granulated sugar
- 3/4 cup vegetable oil
- 3/4 cup HERSHEY'S Cocoa
- 4 eggs
- 2 teaspoons vanilla extract
- 2 1/3 cups all-purpose flour
- 2 teaspoons baking powder
- 1/2 teaspoon salt
- Confectioners' sugar

In large mixer bowl combine granulated sugar and oil. Gradually blend in cocoa. Beat in eggs and vanilla. Combine flour, baking powder and salt; add to cocoa mixture, blending well. Cover; chill at least 6 hours. Heat oven to 350°. Shape dough into 1-inch balls. Roll in confectioners' sugar. Place 2 inches apart on greased cookie sheet. Bake 12 to 14 minutes or until almost no indentation remains when touched. Remove from cookie sheet to wire rack. Cool completely.

About 4 dozen cookies

Chocolate Fruit Bars

- 2 cups vanilla wafer crumbs
- 1/2 cup HERSHEY'S Cocoa
- 3 tablespoons sugar
- 2/3 cup butter or margarine
- 1 cup REESE'S Peanut Butter Chips
- 1/2 cup chopped dates
- 1/2 cup red candied cherries, halved
- 1/2 cup green candied cherries, halved
- 1 can (14 ounces) sweetened condensed milk
- 3/4 cup coarsely broken pecans

Heat oven to 350°. In medium bowl stir together crumbs, cocoa and sugar. With pastry blender blend in butter until well combined. Press mixture onto bottom and 1/2 inch up sides of 13×9×2-inch baking pan. Sprinkle peanut butter chips, then dates and cherries over crust. Pour sweetened condensed milk evenly over fruit. Sprinkle pecans on top; press down lightly. Bake 25 to 30 minutes or until edges of filling are lightly browned and center is bubbly. Cool completely; cover with aluminum foil. Let stand at room temperature about 8 hours before cutting into bars.

About 3 dozen bars

Peanut Butter Glazed Chocolate Cookies

- 1 package (15 ounces) golden sugar cookie mix
- 1/2 cup HERSHEY'S Cocoa
- 1 egg
- 2 tablespoons water
- About 2 cups pecan halves
- Peanut Butter Glaze (recipe follows)

Heat oven to 350°. In medium bowl combine cookie mix (and enclosed flavor packet), cocoa, egg and water; mix with spoon or fork until thoroughly blended. To form base for cookies, on cookie sheet, arrange 3 pecan halves with tips touching in center. Repeat for each cookie. Shape dough into 1-inch balls; gently press one ball onto each pecan cluster until pecans adhere. Bake 8 to 10 minutes or until *almost* set; *do not overbake.* Cool slightly; remove from cookie sheet to wire rack. Cool completely. Place wax paper or foil under rack of cookies. Gently spoon or drizzle thin coating of Peanut Butter Glaze onto each cookie. Allow glaze to set.

About 3 1/2 dozen cookies

Peanut Butter Glaze

In top of double boiler over hot, not boiling, water melt 1 cup REESE'S Peanut Butter Chips and 2 tablespoons shortening (not butter, margarine or oil), stirring constantly to blend; remove from heat and use immediately. (OR in small microwave-safe bowl place peanut chips with shortening. Microwave at HIGH (100%) 45 seconds; stir. If necessary, microwave at HIGH additional 15 seconds or until melted and smooth when stirred. Use immediately.

Signature Brownies

- 1 package (15 ounces) golden sugar cookie mix
- 1/2 cup HERSHEY'S Cocoa
- 1/2 cup HERSHEY'S Syrup
- 1/4 cup butter or margarine, melted
- 1 egg
- 1/2 cup coarsely chopped nuts
- No-Cook Fudge Frosting (recipe follows)

Heat oven to 350°. Grease 8- or 9-inch square baking pan. In medium bowl combine cookie mix (and enclosed flavor packet) and cocoa. Stir in syrup, butter and egg, blending well. Stir in nuts. Spread into pan. Bake 25 to 30 minutes or until wooden pick inserted in center comes out clean. Cool completely. Frost with No-Cook Fudge Frosting. Cut into bars. *About 20 brownies*

No-Cook Fudge Frosting

In small bowl combine 2 cups confectioners' sugar, 1/2 cup HERSHEY'S Syrup, 1/4 cup HERSHEY'S Cocoa, 1/4 cup melted butter or margarine and 1/2 teaspoon vanilla extract; blend well. Use immediately.

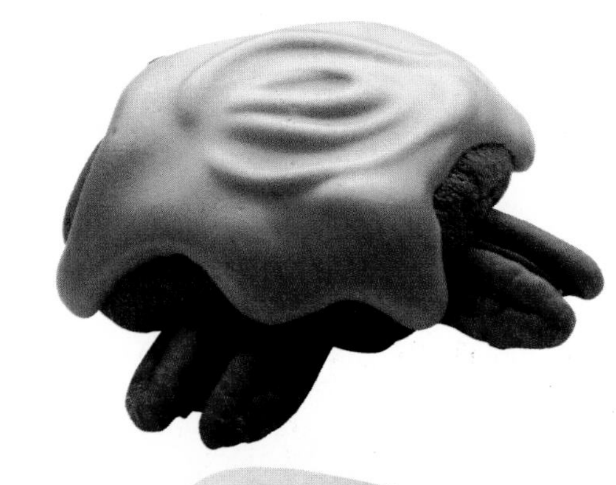

Cherry Cordial Cookies

- 1 package (18.25 ounces) cherry cake mix
- 3/4 cup butter or margarine, softened
- 2 eggs
- 1 cup HERSHEY'S MINI CHIPS Semi-Sweet Chocolate
- MINI CHIPS Glaze (recipe follows)

Heat oven to 350°. In large mixer bowl combine cake mix, butter and eggs; mix well. Stir in MINI CHIPS Chocolate. Drop by rounded teaspoonfuls onto ungreased cookie sheet. Bake 10 to 12 minutes or until almost set. Cool slightly; remove from cookie sheet to wire rack. Cool completely. Drizzle MINI CHIPS Glaze onto cooled cookies; allow to set.

About 4 dozen cookies

Mini Chips Glaze

Microwave Directions: In small microwave-safe bowl place 1 cup HERSHEY'S MINI CHIPS Semi-Sweet Chocolate and 3 tablespoons shortening (not butter, margarine or oil). Microwave at HIGH (100%) 45 seconds; stir. If necessary, microwave at HIGH additional 15 seconds or until melted and smooth when stirred. Use immediately.

Hershey's Great American Chocolate Chip Cookies

- 1 cup butter, softened
- 3/4 cup granulated sugar
- 3/4 cup packed light brown sugar
- 1 teaspoon vanilla extract
- 2 eggs
- 2 1/4 cups all-purpose flour
- 1 teaspoon baking soda
- 1/2 teaspoon salt
- 2 cups (12-ounce package) HERSHEY'S Semi-Sweet Chocolate Chips
- 1 cup chopped nuts (optional)

Heat oven to 375°. In large mixer bowl cream butter, granulated sugar, brown sugar and vanilla until light and fluffy. Add eggs; beat well. Combine flour, baking soda and salt; gradually blend into creamed mixture. Stir in chocolate chips and nuts, if desired. Drop by rounded teaspoonfuls onto ungreased cookie sheet. Bake 8 to 10 minutes or until very lightly browned. Cool slightly; remove from cookie sheet to wire rack. Cool completely.

About 6 dozen cookies

Pan Recipe: Spread batter in greased 15 1/2 × 10 1/2 × 1-inch jelly-roll pan. Bake at 375° for 20 minutes or until lightly browned. Cool completely. Cut into bars.

About 4 dozen bars

Reese's™ Chewy Chocolate Cookies

- 1 1/4 cups butter or margarine, softened
- 2 cups sugar
- 2 eggs
- 2 teaspoons vanilla extract
- 2 cups all-purpose flour
- 3/4 cup HERSHEY'S Cocoa
- 1 teaspoon baking soda
- 1/2 teaspoon salt
- 2 cups (12-ounce package) REESE'S Peanut Butter Chips
- 1/2 cup finely chopped nuts (optional)

Heat oven to 350°. In large mixer bowl cream butter and sugar until light and fluffy. Add eggs and vanilla; beat well. Combine flour, cocoa, baking soda and salt; gradually blend into creamed mixture. Stir in peanut butter chips and nuts, if desired. Drop by teaspoonfuls onto ungreased cookie sheet. Bake 8 to 9 minutes. (Do not overbake; cookies will be soft. They will puff while baking and flatten while cooling). Cool slightly; remove from cookie sheet to wire rack. Cool completely.

About 4 1/2 dozen cookies

Hershey®'s Great American Chocolate Chip Cookies (top) and Reese's Chewy Chocolate Cookies

Chocolate Thumbprint Cookies

- 1/2 cup butter or margarine
- 2/3 cup sugar
- 1 egg, separated
- 2 tablespoons milk
- 1 teaspoon vanilla extract
- 1 cup all-purpose flour
- 1/3 cup HERSHEY'S Cocoa
- 1/4 teaspoon salt
- 1 cup chopped nuts
- Vanilla Filling (recipe follows)
- 26 HERSHEY'S KISSES, unwrapped, or pecan halves or candied cherry halves

In small mixer bowl cream butter, sugar, egg yolk, milk and vanilla. Combine flour, cocoa and salt; blend into creamed mixture. Chill dough at least 1 hour or until firm enough to handle. Heat oven to 350° Shape dough into 1-inch balls. Beat egg white slightly. Dip each ball into egg white; roll in nuts. Place on lightly greased cookie sheet. Press thumb gently in center of each cookie. Bake 10 to 12 minutes or until set. As soon as cookies are removed from oven, spoon about 1/4 teaspoon Filling in thumbprint. Gently press unwrapped KISS in center of each cookie. Carefully remove from cookie sheet to wire rack. Cool completely.

About 2 dozen cookies

Vanilla Filling

In small bowl combine 1/2 cup confectioners' sugar, 1 tablespoon softened butter or margarine, 2 teaspoons milk and 1/4 teaspoon vanilla extract; beat until smooth.

Ultimate Chocolate Brownies

- 3/4 cup HERSHEY'S Cocoa
- 1/2 teaspoon baking soda
- 2/3 cup butter or margarine, melted and divided
- 1/2 cup boiling water
- 2 cups sugar
- 2 eggs
- 1 1/3 cups all-purpose flour
- 1 teaspoon vanilla extract
- 1/4 teaspoon salt
- 1 cup HERSHEY'S Semi-Sweet Chocolate Chips
- One-Bowl Buttercream Frosting (recipe page 191)

Heat oven to 350°. Grease 13×9×2-inch baking pan, or two 8-inch square baking pans. In medium bowl combine cocoa and baking soda. Blend in 1/3 cup butter. Add boiling water; stir until mixture thickens. Stir in sugar, eggs and remaining 1/3 cup butter; stir until smooth. Add flour, vanilla and salt; blend completely. Stir in chocolate chips. Pour into prepared pan(s). Bake 35 to 40 minutes for rectangular pan, 30 to 35 minutes for square pans or until brownies begin to pull away from sides of pan. Cool completely. Frost with One-Bowl Buttercream Frosting. Cut into squares. *About 3 dozen brownies*

Mint Frosted Brownies

Mint Frosted Brownies

- 2 eggs
- 1 cup sugar
- 1/2 cup butter or margarine, melted
- 1 teaspoon vanilla extract
- 2/3 cup all-purpose flour
- 6 tablespoons HERSHEY'S Cocoa
- 1/2 teaspoon baking powder
- 1/4 teaspoon salt
- 1/2 cup chopped walnuts (optional)
- Mint Frosting (recipe follows)
- Walnut halves (optional)

Heat oven to 350°. Grease 8-inch square baking pan. In small mixer bowl beat eggs well; gradually beat in sugar. Blend in butter and vanilla. Combine flour, cocoa, baking powder and salt; add to egg mixture, blending thoroughly. Stir in walnuts, if desired. Spread batter into prepared pan. Bake 20 to 25 minutes or just until brownies begin to pull away from sides of pan. Cool completely. Frost with Mint Frosting. Cut into squares. Garnish with walnut halves, if desired. *16 brownies*

Mint Frosting

- 2 tablespoons butter or margarine, softened
- 1 cup confectioners' sugar
- 1 to 2 tablespoons milk
- 1/4 teaspoon vanilla extract
- 1/8 teaspoon mint extract
- 3 to 4 drops red or green food color

In small mixer bowl combine all ingredients; beat until creamy.

Reese's™ Cookies

- 1 cup shortening OR 3/4 cup butter or margarine
- 1 cup granulated sugar
- 1/2 cup packed light brown sugar
- 1 teaspoon vanilla extract
- 2 eggs
- 2 cups all-purpose flour
- 1 teaspoon baking soda
- 1 cup REESE'S Peanut Butter Chips
- 1 cup HERSHEY'S Semi-Sweet or Milk Chocolate Chips

Heat oven to 350°. In large mixer bowl cream shortening or butter, granulated sugar, brown sugar and vanilla. Add eggs; beat well. Combine flour and baking soda; blend into creamed mixture. Stir in peanut butter chips and chocolate chips. Drop by rounded teaspoonfuls onto ungreased cookie sheet. Bake 10 to 12 minutes or until very lightly browned. Cool slightly; remove from cookie sheet to wire rack. Cool completely.

About 5 dozen cookies

Peanut Butter Chips and Jelly Bars

- 1 $1/2$ cups all-purpose flour
- $1/2$ cup sugar
- $3/4$ teaspoon baking powder
- $1/2$ cup butter or margarine
- 1 egg, beaten
- $3/4$ cup grape jelly
- 1 cup REESE'S Peanut Butter Chips, divided

Heat oven to 375°. Grease 9-inch square baking pan. In medium bowl combine flour, sugar and baking powder; cut in butter with pastry blender or fork to form coarse crumbs. Add egg; blend well. Reserve half of mixture; press remaining mixture onto bottom of prepared pan. Spread jelly evenly over crust. Sprinkle $1/2$ cup peanut butter chips over jelly. Combine remaining crumb mixture with remaining $1/2$ cup chips; sprinkle over top. Bake 25 to 30 minutes or until lightly browned. Cool completely. Cut into bars.

About 1 $1/2$ dozen bars

Chocoroons

- 5 $1/3$ cups (14-ounce package) shredded coconut
- $2/3$ cup all-purpose flour
- $1/4$ teaspoon salt
- 1 can (14 ounces) sweetened condensed milk
- 1 cup HERSHEY'S Semi-Sweet Chocolate Chips or MINI CHIPS
- 1 cup coarsely chopped walnuts, pecans or almonds

Heat oven to 300°. In large bowl combine coconut, flour and salt. Stir in sweetened condensed milk, blending well. Stir in chocolate chips and nuts. Drop by rounded teaspoonfuls onto generously greased cookie sheet. Bake 12 to 14 minutes or until bottoms begin to brown. Immediately remove from cookie sheet to wire rack. Cool completely.

About 4 dozen cookies

Peanut Butter Chips and Jelly Bars

Double Fudge Saucepan Brownies

- 1/2 cup sugar
- 2 tablespoons butter or margarine
- 2 tablespoons water
- 2 cups (12-ounce package) HERSHEY'S Semi-Sweet Chocolate Chips, divided
- 2 eggs, slightly beaten
- 1 teaspoon vanilla extract
- 2/3 cup all-purpose flour
- 1/4 teaspoon baking soda
- 1/4 teaspoon salt
- 1/2 cup chopped nuts (optional)

Heat oven to 325°. Grease 9-inch square baking pan. In medium saucepan over low heat cook sugar, butter and water, stirring constantly, until mixture comes to boil. Remove from heat; immediately add 1 cup chocolate chips, stirring until chips are melted. Stir in eggs and vanilla until blended. Combine flour, baking soda and salt; stir into chocolate mixture. Stir in remaining 1 cup chips and nuts, if desired. Pour into prepared pan. Bake 25 to 30 minutes or until brownies begin to pull away from sides of pan. Cool completely. Cut into bars.

About 1 1/2 dozen brownies

Ornament Cookies

Ornament Cookies

- 1/2 cup butter or margarine
- 3/4 cup sugar
- 1 egg
- 3/4 teaspoon peppermint extract
- 1 tablespoon milk
- 1 1/2 cups all-purpose flour
- 1/3 cup HERSHEY'S Cocoa
- 1/2 teaspoon baking powder
- 1/8 teaspoon salt
- Decorator Frosting (recipe follows)
- Colored sprinkles (optional)

In large mixer bowl cream butter, sugar, egg, peppermint extract and milk until light and fluffy. Combine flour, cocoa, baking powder and salt; add to creamed mixture. Mix until well blended. Divide dough into quarters; wrap tightly. Chill 2 to 3 hours. Heat oven to 325°. On lightly floured surface roll out dough, one quarter at a time, to 1/8 inch thickness. Cut dough with cookie cutters. With wooden pick pierce hole at top of each cookie for hanging on tree. Place cookies 1 inch apart on ungreased cookie sheet. Bake 8 to 10 minutes or until firm. Carefully remove from cookie sheet to wire rack. Cool completely. Decorate using Decorator Frosting and colored sprinkles, if desired.

About 2 dozen cookies

Decorator Frosting

In small mixer bowl combine 2 1/2 to 3 cups confectioners' sugar, 2 egg whites and 1/4 teaspoon peppermint extract. Beat on high speed until stiff. Stir in 1 or 2 drops food color, if desired.

Deep Dish Brownies

- 3/4 cup butter or margarine, melted
- 1 1/2 cups sugar
- 1 1/2 teaspoons vanilla extract
- 3 eggs
- 3/4 cup all-purpose flour
- 1/2 cup HERSHEY'S Cocoa
- 1/2 teaspoon baking powder
- 1/2 teaspoon salt

Heat oven to 350°. Grease 8-inch square baking pan. In medium bowl blend butter, sugar and vanilla. Add eggs; using spoon, beat well. Combine flour, cocoa, baking powder and salt; gradually add to egg mixture, beating until well blended. Spread into prepared pan. Bake 40 to 45 minutes or until brownies begin to pull away from sides of pan. Cool completely; cut into squares. *16 brownies*

Variation: Stir 1 cup REESE'S Peanut Butter Chips or HERSHEY'S Semi-Sweet Chocolate Chips into batter.

Sour Cream Chocolate Cookies

- 2 eggs
- 1 cup granulated sugar
- 1 cup packed light brown sugar
- 1 teaspoon vanilla extract
- 1 cup dairy sour cream
- 1/2 cup butter or margarine, melted
- 1/2 cup shortening, melted
- 2 1/2 cups all-purpose flour
- 1 cup HERSHEY'S Cocoa
- 1 teaspoon baking powder
- 1/2 teaspoon baking soda
- 1 cup chopped walnuts

Heat oven to 325°. In large mixer bowl beat eggs, granulated sugar, brown sugar and vanilla. Blend in sour cream, butter and shortening. Combine flour, cocoa, baking powder and baking soda; add to sugar mixture. Stir in walnuts. Drop by tablespoonfuls onto greased cookie sheet. Bake 10 to 12 minutes or just until set. Cool slightly; remove from cookie sheet. Cool on wire rack.

About 4 dozen cookies

Cocoa Kiss Cookies

Cocoa Kiss Cookies

- 1 cup butter or margarine, softened
- 2/3 cup granulated sugar
- 1 teaspoon vanilla extract
- 1 2/3 cups all-purpose flour
- 1/4 cup HERSHEY'S Cocoa
- 1 cup finely chopped pecans
- 54 HERSHEY'S KISSES (9-ounce package), unwrapped
- Confectioners' sugar

In large mixer bowl cream butter, granulated sugar and vanilla until light and fluffy. Combine flour and cocoa; blend into creamed mixture. Add pecans; beat on low speed until well blended. Chill dough 1 hour or until firm enough to handle. Heat oven to 375°. Mold scant tablespoon of dough around each unwrapped KISS, covering KISS completely. Shape into balls; place on ungreased cookie sheet. Bake 10 to 12 minutes or until almost set; cool slightly. Remove from cookie sheet to wire rack. Cool completely. Roll in confectioners' sugar.

About 4 1/2 dozen cookies

BEVERAGES

Rich cocoas to warm you in winter, plus frothy favorites to cool you off in summer.

From left to right: Irish Cocoa, Cocoa-Banana Shake and Hot Cocoa (recipes page 176)

Irish Cocoa

- 6 tablespoons sugar
- 3 tablespoons HERSHEY'S Cocoa
- Dash salt
- 1/4 cup hot water
- 3 cups milk
- 6 tablespoons Irish whiskey
- 1/2 cup chilled whipping cream, whipped

In medium saucepan combine sugar, cocoa and salt; stir in water. Cook over medium heat, stirring constantly, until mixture boils. Boil and stir 2 minutes. Add milk; stir and heat to serving temperature. *Do not boil.* Remove from heat. Pour 1 tablespoon whiskey in each cup or goblet. Fill cup with hot cocoa; stir to blend. Serve hot, topped with whipped cream.

About six 6-ounce servings

Cocoa-Banana Shake

- 1 ripe, medium banana
- 1/4 cup HERSHEY'S Cocoa
- 1/4 cup honey
- 1/4 cup hot water
- 2 cups cold milk
- 1 cup vanilla ice cream

Slice banana into blender container. Add cocoa, honey and water; cover and blend until smooth. Add milk; cover and blend. Add ice cream; cover and blend until smooth. Serve immediately.

About four 8-ounce servings

Hot Cocoa

- 1/2 cup sugar
- 1/4 cup HERSHEY'S Cocoa
- Dash salt
- 1/3 cup hot water
- 4 cups (1 quart) milk
- 3/4 teaspoon vanilla extract
- Sweetened whipped cream (optional)

In medium saucepan combine sugar, cocoa and salt; blend in water. Cook over medium heat, stirring constantly, until mixture boils. Boil and stir 2 minutes. Add milk; stir and heat to serving temperature. *Do not boil.* Remove from heat; add vanilla. Beat with rotary beater or wire whisk until foamy. Serve hot, topped with sweetened whipped cream, if desired.

About six 6-ounce servings

VARIATIONS

Spiced Cocoa: Add 1/8 teaspoon ground cinnamon and 1/8 teaspoon ground nutmeg with vanilla.

Citrus Cocoa: Add 1/2 teaspoon orange extract or 2 to 3 tablespoons orange liqueur with vanilla.

Swiss Mocha: Add 2 to 2 1/2 teaspoons powdered instant coffee with vanilla.

Mint Cocoa: Add 1/2 teaspoon mint extract, or 3 tablespoons crushed hard peppermint candy, or 2 to 3 tablespoons white creme de menthe with vanilla.

Cocoa au Lait: Omit whipped cream. Spoon 2 tablespoons softened vanilla ice cream on top of each cup of cocoa at serving time.

Slim-Trim Cocoa: Omit sugar. Combine cocoa, salt and water; substitute skim milk. Proceed as above. With vanilla, stir in sugar substitute with sweetening equivalence of 1/2 cup sugar.

Microwave Single Serving: In 8-ounce microwave-safe mug, combine 2 heaping teaspoons sugar and 1 heaping teaspoon HERSHEY'S Cocoa. Add 2 teaspoons cold milk; stir until smooth. Fill mug with milk; microwave at HIGH (100%) 1 to 1 1/2 minutes or just until hot. Stir to blend before serving.

Chocolate Strawberry Cooler

1/2 cup sliced strawberries
2 tablespoons sugar
1 tablespoon HERSHEY'S Cocoa
1 cup milk, divided
1/2 cup cold club soda, freshly opened
Ice cream or whipped cream
2 fresh strawberries (optional)

In blender container combine sliced strawberries, sugar, cocoa and 1/2 cup milk; cover and blend until smooth. Add remaining 1/2 cup milk and club soda; cover and blend. Pour into 2 glasses. Garnish with ice cream or whipped cream and strawberry, if desired. Serve immediately.

About two 8-ounce servings

Chocolate Strawberry Cooler

Spiced Mocha (from mix)

Hot Cocoa Mix

2 cups non-fat dry milk powder
3/4 cup sugar
1/2 cup HERSHEY'S Cocoa
1/2 cup powdered non-dairy creamer
Dash salt

In large bowl combine all ingredients; blend well. Store mix in tightly covered container.

3 3/4 cups mix (about fifteen 6-ounce servings)

Single serving: Place 1/4 cup mix in heatproof cup or mug; stir in 3/4 cup boiling water. Serve hot, topped with marshmallows, if desired.

Spiced Mocha Mix

1 cup sugar
1 cup nonfat dry milk powder
1/2 cup powdered non-dairy creamer
1/2 cup HERSHEY'S Cocoa
3 tablespoons powdered instant coffee
1/2 teaspoon ground allspice
1/4 teaspoon ground cinnamon
Dash salt

In large bowl combine all ingredients. Store in airtight container.

2 1/2 cups mix (12 to 14 servings)

For Single Serving: Place 3 tablespoons mix in mug or cup; add 3/4 cup boiling water. Stir until mix is dissolved. Top with marshmallows, if desired. Serve immediately.

Choco Peanut Butter Shake

3/4 cup cold milk
1/4 cup creamy peanut butter
3 tablespoons HERSHEY'S Cocoa
1 tablespoon marshmallow creme
2 cups vanilla ice cream

In blender container place milk, peanut butter, cocoa and marshmallow creme. Cover; blend. Add ice cream. Cover; blend until smooth. Serve immediately.

About three 6-ounce servings

New York Chocolate Egg Cream

- 1/4 cup Cocoa Syrup (recipe follows)
- 1/4 cup light cream
- 1/2 cup club soda, freshly opened

All ingredients should be cold. Measure syrup into tall glass; stir in cream to blend. Slowly pour club soda down side of glass, stirring constantly. Serve immediately.

One 8-ounce serving

Cocoa Syrup

- 1 1/2 cups sugar
- 3/4 cup HERSHEY'S Cocoa
- Dash salt
- 1 cup hot water
- 2 teaspoons vanilla extract

In medium saucepan combine sugar, cocoa and salt. Gradually add water, stirring to keep mixture smooth. Cook over medium heat, stirring constantly, until mixture boils; boil and stir 3 minutes. Remove from heat; stir in vanilla. Cool. Pour into heatproof container; cover and chill. Use as topping for ice cream and desserts, or for chocolate-flavored drinks.

About 2 cups syrup

Quick Blender Hot Chocolate

- 3 cups milk, heated to boiling
- 1 cup HERSHEY'S MINI CHIPS Semi-Sweet Chocolate

In blender container place milk and MINI CHIPS Chocolate. Cover; blend until smooth. Serve immediately.

About four 6-ounce servings

Mocha Delight

- 1 cup milk
- 1 tablespoon HERSHEY'S Cocoa
- 1 tablespoon sugar
- 1/2 teaspoon powdered instant coffee
- 3 to 4 drops almond extract (optional)
- 1/2 cup cold vanilla ice cream

In blender container combine milk, cocoa, sugar, instant coffee and almond extract, if desired; cover and blend. Add ice cream; cover and blend until smooth. Serve immediately.

About two 6-ounce servings

Chocolate Ice Cream Soda

- 3 tablespoons HERSHEY'S Syrup
- 1/4 cup cold ginger ale or club soda, freshly opened
- 2 scoops vanilla ice cream
- Additional cold ginger ale or club soda

In 12-ounce glass stir together syrup and 1/4 cup ginger ale. Add ice cream. Fill glass with additional ginger ale. Serve immediately.

1 soda

Cocoa Fruit Breakfast Drink

- 1 container (8 ounces) strawberry yogurt
- 1 1/4 cups cold milk
- 1 cup fresh strawberries, sliced
- 1 ripe, medium banana, sliced
- 3 tablespoons HERSHEY'S Cocoa
- 2 tablespoons honey

In blender container place all ingredients. Cover; blend until smooth.

About five 6-ounce servings

Chocolate Shake

- 2 cups cold milk
- 2 cups vanilla ice cream, divided
- 3/4 cup HERSHEY'S Syrup

In blender container place milk, 1 cup ice cream and syrup. Cover; blend until smooth. Pour into glasses; top with scoops of remaining ice cream.

About three 10-ounce servings

VARIATIONS

Before blending, add one of the following:

- 1 ripe, medium banana, sliced
- 2/3 cup drained, canned peach slices
- 1/2 teaspoon mint extract
- 1/2 cup crushed, sweetened strawberries

From left to right: Cocoa Fruit Breakfast Drink, Chocolate Shake and Double Chocolate Malt (recipe page 182)

Double Chocolate Malt

- 1/2 cup cold milk
- 1/4 cup HERSHEY'S Syrup
- 2 tablespoons chocolate malted milk powder
- 2 cups vanilla ice cream, softened

In blender container place milk, syrup and malted milk powder. Cover; blend. Add ice cream. Cover; blend until smooth. Serve immediately.

About three 6-ounce servings

VARIATION
Triple Chocolate Malt: Substitute chocolate ice cream for vanilla ice cream.

Hot Cocoa For A Crowd

- 1 1/2 cups sugar
- 1 1/4 cups HERSHEY'S Cocoa
- 1/2 teaspoon salt
- 3/4 cup hot water
- 4 quarts (1 gallon) milk
- 1 tablespoon vanilla extract

In 6-quart saucepan combine sugar, cocoa and salt; gradually add hot water. Cook over medium heat, stirring constantly, until mixture boils. Boil and stir 2 minutes. Add milk; heat to serving temperature, stirring occasionally. *Do not boil.* Remove from heat; add vanilla. Serve hot.

About twenty-two 6-ounce servings

Hot Merry Mocha

- 6 tablespoons HERSHEY'S Cocoa
- 1 to 2 tablespoons powdered instant coffee
- 1/8 teaspoon salt
- 6 cups hot water
- 1 can (14 ounces) sweetened condensed milk
- Sweetened whipped cream (optional)

In 4-quart saucepan combine cocoa, instant coffee and salt; stir in water. Cook over medium heat, stirring occasionally, until mixture boils. Stir in sweetened condensed milk; heat thoroughly. *Do not boil.* Beat with rotary beater or wire whisk until foamy. Serve hot, topped with sweetened whipped cream, if desired.

About ten 6-ounce servings

VARIATION
Minted Hot Chocolate: Follow directions above omitting instant coffee. Stir in 1/4 to 1/2 teaspoon mint extract before beating. Serve with candy cane for stirrer, if desired.

Cappuccino Cooler

- 1 1/2 cups cold coffee
- 1 1/2 cups chocolate ice cream
- 1/4 cup HERSHEY'S Syrup
- Crushed ice
- Whipped cream

In blender container place coffee, ice cream and syrup. Cover; blend until smooth. Serve immediately over crushed ice. Garnish with whipped cream.

About four 6-ounce servings

Chocolate Egg Nog

4 cups milk, divided
4 eggs, separated
1/3 cup HERSHEY'S Cocoa
1 can (14 ounces) sweetened condensed milk
1 teaspoon vanilla extract
1/4 teaspoon salt
2 teaspoons brandy extract*
1 teaspoon rum extract*
Grated chocolate

In blender container combine 1 cup milk, egg yolks, cocoa, sweetened condensed milk, vanilla and salt. Cover and blend on high speed until smooth, about 30 seconds. Pour mixture into large bowl; stir in remaining 3 cups milk and extracts, blending well. Beat egg whites until soft peaks form; gently fold into milk mixture. Chill thoroughly. Stir well before serving. Sprinkle with grated chocolate.

About eight 6-ounce servings

*Note: 1/2 cup brandy or bourbon may be substituted for extracts.

SAUCES, TOPPINGS & FROSTINGS

Try these delicious sauces, toppings and more with your favorite dessert.

From left to right: Fudge Frosting, Quick Hot Fudge Sauce and Chocolate Whipped Cream (recipes page 186)

Fudge Frosting

1 cup sugar
1/4 cup HERSHEY'S Cocoa
1/2 cup milk
1/4 cup butter or margarine
2 tablespoons light corn syrup
Dash salt
1 1/2 cups confectioners' sugar
1 teaspoon vanilla extract

In medium saucepan combine sugar and cocoa. Stir in milk, butter, corn syrup and salt. Cook over medium heat, stirring constantly, until mixture comes to a full boil. Boil, stirring occasionally, 3 minutes. Remove from heat; cool to lukewarm. In small mixer bowl place confectioners' sugar; stir in chocolate mixture and vanilla. Beat until spreading consistency.

About 2 cups frosting

Sweetened Whipped Cream

1 cup chilled whipping cream
1 to 2 tablespoons confectioners' sugar
1/2 teaspoon vanilla extract

In small mixer bowl combine cream, confectioners' sugar and vanilla; beat until stiff. Serve cold.

About 2 cups topping

Chocolate Whipped Cream

In small mixer bowl combine 1/2 cup sugar and 1/4 cup HERSHEY'S Cocoa. Add 1 cup chilled whipping cream and 1 teaspoon vanilla extract; beat until stiff. Serve cold.

About 2 cups topping

Quick Hot Fudge Sauce

2 tablespoons butter or margarine
1/3 cup HERSHEY'S Cocoa
1 can (14 ounces) sweetened condensed milk
2 tablespoons water
1 teaspoon vanilla extract

In heavy 2-quart saucepan combine all ingredients except vanilla. Cook over medium heat, stirring constantly with whisk, until sauce is smooth and slightly thickened, about 5 minutes. Remove from heat; stir in vanilla. Serve warm over ice cream or desserts. *About 1 1/2 cups sauce*

Microwave Directions: In medium microwave-safe bowl place butter. Microwave at HIGH (100%) 30 to 45 seconds or until melted; stir in cocoa until smooth. Blend in sweetened condensed milk and water. Microwave at HIGH 1 minute; stir. Microwave at HIGH 1 to 2 additional minutes, stirring with whisk after each minute, or until mixture is smooth and warm. Stir in vanilla. Serve as directed.

Chocolate Peanut Butter Sauce

1/2 cup HERSHEY'S Chocolate Fudge Topping
1/2 cup HERSHEY'S Syrup
1/4 cup creamy peanut butter

In small saucepan place all ingredients. Cook over low heat, stirring constantly, until mixture is warm. Serve immediately over ice cream or other desserts.

About 1 1/4 cups sauce

Chocolate Sour Cream Frosting

- 1/2 cup butter or margarine
- 1/2 cup HERSHEY'S Cocoa
- 3 cups confectioners' sugar
- 1/2 cup dairy sour cream
- 2 teaspoons vanilla extract

In small saucepan over low heat melt butter. Add cocoa and stir constantly until mixture is smooth and slightly thickened. Transfer to small mixer bowl; cool slightly. Add confectioners' sugar alternately with sour cream; beat to spreading consistency. Stir in vanilla.

About 2 1/2 cups frosting

Mocha Butter Frosting

- 1 teaspoon powdered instant coffee
- 1 teaspoon hot water
- 1/4 cup butter or margarine, softened
- 3 tablespoons HERSHEY'S Cocoa
- 1 teaspoon vanilla extract
- 1 egg, beaten
- 2 cups confectioners' sugar

In small mixer bowl dissolve instant coffee in water. Blend in butter, cocoa and vanilla. Blend in egg. Gradually beat in confectioners' sugar until well blended. Add water, 1 teaspoon at a time, if necessary, until desired consistency.

About 1 3/4 cups frosting

Fudgey Chocolate Fondue

- 1/2 cup butter or margarine
- 1/2 cup HERSHEY'S Cocoa
- 3/4 cup sugar
- 1/2 cup evaporated milk or light cream
- 1 teaspoon vanilla extract

In small saucepan over low heat melt butter. Remove from heat; immediately stir in cocoa. Add sugar and evaporated milk; cook over low heat, stirring constantly, until sugar is dissolved and mixture is smooth. Remove from heat; stir in vanilla. Serve warm with selection of fruit, marshmallows or small pieces of cake or cookies.

About 1 1/2 cups fondue

Fudgey Chocolate Fondue

Peanut Butter Sauce

1 cup REESE'S Peanut Butter Chips
1/3 cup milk
1/4 cup whipping cream
1/4 teaspoon vanilla extract

In small saucepan place peanut butter chips, milk and whipping cream. Cook over low heat, stirring constantly, until chips are melted and mixture is smooth. Remove from heat; stir in vanilla. Serve warm. Cover; refrigerate leftover sauce.

About 1 cup sauce

To reheat: Place sauce in small saucepan. Stir constantly over low heat until warm. Add additional milk or whipping cream for desired consistency.

Mocha Satin Sauce

1/2 cup butter
1 cup sugar
1 cup whipping cream
1/3 cup HERSHEY'S Cocoa
1 teaspoon powdered instant coffee
1 teaspoon vanilla extract

In small saucepan over low heat melt butter. Stir in sugar, whipping cream and cocoa. Cook over medium heat, stirring frequently, until mixture begins to boil. Reduce heat; simmer 5 minutes. Remove from heat; stir in instant coffee and vanilla. Serve warm or cool. Cover; refrigerate leftover sauce.

About 2 cups sauce

To reheat: Place sauce in small saucepan. Stir constantly over low heat until warm.

From left to right: Peanut Butter Sauce, Mocha Satin Sauce and Bittersweet Chocolate Sauce

Bittersweet Chocolate Sauce

2 cups (12-ounce package) HERSHEY'S Semi-Sweet Chocolate Chips
2 squares (2 ounces) HERSHEY'S Unsweetened Baking Chocolate, chopped
1 cup whipping cream
1 1/2 teaspoons vanilla extract

In top of double boiler over hot, not boiling, water place chocolate chips, baking chocolate and whipping cream. Cook, stirring frequently, until chocolate is melted and mixture is smooth. Remove from heat; stir in vanilla. Serve warm. Cover; refrigerate leftover sauce.

About 2 cups sauce

To reheat: Place sauce in small saucepan. Stir constantly over low heat until warm.

Cocoa Cheese Frosting

3 packages (3 ounces each) cream cheese, softened
1/3 cup butter or margarine
5 cups confectioners' sugar
1 cup HERSHEY'S Cocoa
5 to 7 tablespoons light cream

In large mixer bowl blend cream cheese and butter. Combine confectioners' sugar and cocoa; add alternately with light cream to cream cheese mixture. Beat until spreading consistency.

About 3 cups frosting

Creamy Chocolate Frosting

3 squares (3 ounces) HERSHEY'S Unsweetened Baking Chocolate
1 cup miniature marshmallows
1/2 cup butter or margarine, softened
1/3 cup milk
2 1/2 cups confectioners' sugar
1/2 teaspoon vanilla extract

In top of double boiler over hot, not boiling, water melt baking chocolate. Add marshmallows; stir frequently until marshmallows are melted. Pour mixture into small mixer bowl. Beat in butter and milk until mixture is smooth. Add confectioners' sugar and vanilla; beat to desired consistency.

About 2 1/2 cups frosting

Fluffy Cocoa Topping

2 packages (3 ounces each) cream cheese, softened
1/3 cup sugar
1/4 cup HERSHEY'S Cocoa
3 tablespoons milk
2 cups frozen non-dairy whipped topping, thawed

In small mixer bowl beat cream cheese, sugar and cocoa. Add milk; beat until smooth and fluffy. Stir in whipped topping. Serve as topping for unfrosted cakes.

About 2 1/4 cups topping

Cocoa Glaze

- 1 cup whipping cream
- 1 tablespoon light corn syrup
- 1 cup HERSHEY'S Cocoa
- 1 cup sugar
- 2 tablespoons butter or margarine
- 1 tablespoon vanilla extract

In heavy 2-quart saucepan stir together cream and corn syrup. Sift cocoa and sugar together; stir into cream mixture. Add butter. Cook over low heat, stirring constantly, 6 to 8 minutes or until butter melts and mixture is smooth; *do not boil.* Remove from heat; stir in vanilla. Use glaze while warm.

About 2 cups glaze

Note: Glaze can be stored in airtight container in refrigerator up to 2 weeks. Reheat over low heat, stirring constantly.

Quick Black Forest Fondue

2 jars (12 ounces each) maraschino cherries, with stems
1 cup HERSHEY'S Milk Chocolate Chips
1 cup HERSHEY'S Semi-Sweet Chocolate Chips
1 can (5 ounces) evaporated milk
1/4 to 1/2 teaspoon almond extract

Drain cherries; set aside. (If desired, cherries may be placed on flat tray in freezer at least 1 hour before serving.) In medium saucepan combine chocolate chips and evaporated milk; stir lightly. Cook over very low heat, stirring constantly, until chocolate is melted and mixture is smooth. Remove from heat; stir in almond extract. Pour into fondue pot or chafing dish; dip cherries into warm fondue.

About 1 1/2 cups fondue

Chocolate Whipped Cream Frosting

2 tablespoons confectioners' sugar
1 tablespoon HERSHEY'S Cocoa
1 1/2 cups chilled whipping cream
1/4 cup HERSHEY'S Syrup

In small mixer bowl stir together confectioners' sugar and cocoa. Stir in whipping cream. Beat until stiff; blend in syrup. Chill until desired consistency.

About 2 1/2 cups frosting

One-Bowl Buttercream Frosting

6 tablespoons butter or margarine, softened
HERSHEY'S Cocoa:
1/3 cup for light flavor
1/2 cup for medium flavor
3/4 cup for dark flavor
2 2/3 cups confectioners' sugar
1/3 cup milk
1 teaspoon vanilla extract

In small mixer bowl cream butter. Blend in cocoa and confectioners' sugar alternately with milk; beat to spreading consistency (additional milk may be needed). Blend in vanilla. *About 2 cups frosting*

Peanut Butter Glaze

1 cup REESE'S Peanut Butter Chips
2 tablespoons shortening (not butter, margarine or oil)

In top of double boiler over hot, not boiling, water, melt peanut butter chips and shortening, stirring constantly to blend. Remove from heat; use immediately.

About 1 cup

Microwave Directions: In small microwave-safe bowl place peanut butter chips and shortening. Microwave at HIGH (100%) 45 seconds; stir. If necessary, microwave at HIGH additional 15 seconds or until melted and smooth when stirred. Use immediately.

235
260
273
300
°F
370
390